Narcissistic Mothers

*How To Set Boundaries and Protect Yourself
From Emotional Abuse, CPTSD and Toxic
Shame*

Melanie Parker

Table of Contents

Introduction

We all have the misconception that a narcissistic relationship is exclusive to romantic partnerships, such as a relationship between a boyfriend and girlfriend or a husband and wife.

However, unfortunately, many people are susceptible to suffering severe emotional or psychological pain at the hands of a narcissistic parent.

This book, therefore, was written to educate you on how to emotionally recover from the grief and hurt caused by being raised by narcissistic parents, specifically, a narcissistic mother, so you can set yourself free.

It is my opinion that being brought up by a narcissistic parent is an experience that is far more detrimental than being married to or being romantically involved with a narcissist. Because if a person is in a relationship, they have the ability to leave their abusive partner and free themselves of their influence, even if doing so is challenging; however, a child cannot escape a narcissistic mother.

As a result, they frequently remain living with their mother until they reach adulthood. This causes significant damage.

It also raises an important question: how can you tell whether you were raised by a narcissistic mother? To answer this, first, you must understand who or what exactly is a narcissist and how do you recognize their characteristics?

Chapter 1:
Is My Mother A Narcissist?

I n this first chapter, I'll talk about the relationship between a mother and daughter when the mother is narcissistic. I'll also discuss the concept of **maternal narcissism**. This is something that counselors and other clinical workers witness all the time.

Then, I'll examine the nine signs of a narcissistic mother to explain maternal narcissism in detail. However, some of these signs would also apply to mother-son, father-son, and father-daughter relationships. This brings us to how to look at narcissistic parents in general. I'll talk about parenting styles after talking about narcissistic parents.

After that, I'll examine the characteristics of a narcissistic mother and what it means to have a narcissistic mother.

But first, let's examine the core concept of this book: narcissism.

What Is Narcissism?

Narcissism is a personality trait that includes the traits of self-centeredness and the overwhelming desire for validation and admiration. In general, there are two types of narcissism. There is **overt narcissism**, which characterizes someone who is socially dominant, arrogant, and hard to criticize.

It is different from **vulnerable narcissism**, which is marked by shame, hypersensitivity to criticism, and easy to anger. It is less obvious to detect than overt narcissism and is sometimes referred to as **covert narcissism**.

What Causes Narcissism?

Narcissism is thought to be caused by genes and the environment, much like all other personality disorders. A significant amount of research has been conducted to determine the significance of these two types of narcissism.

Selfishness has a heritability rate of between 47 and 64%, whereas the influence of the environment is between 36% and 53%. Personally, I assume that the influence of both is about 50/50.

One of the questions I am frequently asked in my profession is whether or not a narcissistic mother can make her daughter selfish. This worries many of my clients because most people don't want to be self-centered, and they worry that being around a narcissist, especially a figure of significant influence like a mother, could make them narcissistic too.

There are a few ideas about how this might happen. We know that narcissistic parenting can result in the development of narcissism among children, but we don't know how it happens. One theory states that too much or too little gratification can result in the development of narcissism.

In the **too much theory**, the child expects a level of satisfaction that they don't attain in real life. Therefore, they develop it on their own. According to the two little theory, this leads to narcissism.

It is also believed that the very nature of narcissistic parents can cause narcissism; however, research results are mixed in this area, which brings me to parenting styles. This topic is interesting, especially regarding the narcissistic mother because it examines how the mother and father contribute to the development of narcissism.

Parenting Styles and the Development of Narcissism

Parenting styles can be categorized into four styles: authoritarian, authoritative, permissive, and indifferent.

Authoritarian: When a parent is authoritarian, they want to maintain control of their child. Obedience is expected without the need for an explanation. Therefore, the parent tells the child what to do, but not why they should do it. The parent is strict and demands obedience. When a parent punishes a child, the child is expected to obey. This is how submission is warranted.

Authoritative: The authoritative parent tries to change a child's behavior by presenting reasons and explanations for establishing rules so that the child always possesses an understanding of why they can and cannot do certain actions. This kind of parent is assertive, but not too much. They don't get in the way of the child's development, believe that the child has rights of their own, and consider what the child thinks.

Permissive: A permissive parent raises their kids with a lot of love. They are soft, find it hard to punish their kids and don't want them to grow up out of childhood.

Indifferent: The indifferent parent allows the child to figure out how to solve problems independently. The child is told to be able to do the things they want to do. The parent doesn't help them in any way.

Each of these styles of raising a child has its advantages and disadvantages; however, the authoritative style is usually considered to be the healthiest for the child.

To determine how narcissistic traits potentially developed, examine the individual's unhealthy behaviors and compare them to the commonly recognized traits of narcissism and how it might have started.

The Development of the Vulnerable Narcissist

Research shows that when a mother raises a child in an authoritarian style, the child is more likely to develop into a vulnerable narcissist. When a mother raises a child in a permissive or authoritative style, this is bad for a vulnerable narcissist. This means that as the mother uses these styles, vulnerable narcissism in the child diminishes. Therefore, it doesn't make people more likely to be vulnerable narcissists. The indifferent style has nothing to do with it, so if the mother uses it, we don't see any difference between the child and vulnerable narcissism.

The Development of the Grandiose Narcissist

Concerning **grandiose narcissism**, we can see that the mother's parenting style is not related to the development of grandiose narcissism in the child. This means a mother is not the cause of grandiose narcissism; however, there are several things a father can do that could cause the development of grandiose narcissism.

If we look at this from the father's point of view, we can see that the authoritarian, indifferent and permissive parenting styles are linked to the development of grandiose narcissism when used by the father.

Therefore, it can be concluded that having narcissistic parents can give rise to the development of a child narcissist; however, that's not the only problem. Next, I'll talk about what happens when a mother is too self-centered. Then, I will talk about the traits of a narcissistic mother, a common issue in my clinical work.

How To Recognize a Narcissistic Mother

Sign 1 — She Turns the Conversation to Herself

For example, the daughter wants to talk to her mother about a problem she is having, but the conversation turns into one concerning the mother's problem, which is always bigger, worse, and more important. Sometimes, the daughter is even to blame for it. If the daughter says, "This is also pretty common" or "I can't seem to get things done, the narcissistic mother will most likely respond, "I know how you feel. It's exactly how I felt when I was trying to raise you, but you wouldn't listen. You wanted to do things your way all the time. You never understood how I felt."

Sign 2 — She Openly Displays Love for Male Figures Over Her Daughter

This is shown in many ways: she might flirt with her daughter's boyfriend in front of her daughter; she will force the daughter to compete for the love of her daughter's father or step-father; she will ensure the daughter will feel as though she will never be good enough for her or as successful as her. In a nutshell, the mother treats her daughter as though she were less important, or, more precisely, like a less important version of herself, one that was never quite as good as she.

Sign 3 — She Makes Her Daughter Feel Like She Is a Burden

She gives you the impression that being with her is putting pressure on her or that you are an emotional strain. You could experience guilt or shame just for being who you are

Sign 4 — She Doesn't Protect Her Daughter From Dangerous People or From Someone in the Family Who Hurts Them

Sometimes, the narcissistic mother even protects the individual hurting the daughter. They don't care if their daughters are mistreated, and in some ways, they might even enjoy it. They convince themselves that their daughter is being punished for being a bad daughter.

Sign 5 — She Is Emotionally Unavailable

This means she doesn't want to or doesn't know how to talk about feelings. I think the wrong kind of emotional availability is linked to this. It's not that they aren't available, but they are available in the wrong way. When the daughter says, "This other person did something that made me angry and hurt," the mother will respond, "You might be dangerous or violent. I always knew you were like that, so I could never really put my faith in you. I can't say you'll be safe."

In a way, it's the same as being emotionally unavailable because the daughter doesn't want to discuss her feelings because they are perceived very differently from her mother's point of view. This sign shows that feelings aren't being validated or at least, not very much.

Sign 6 — She Is Controlling and Manipulative

When the daughter falls short, there is much drama. For example, if the daughter gets into minor trouble at school, the mother might say, "I am hurt, disappointed, shocked, or disgusted." This is an example of blowing something small out of proportion and making it about themselves again.

We also sometimes see a disappointed look instead of a clear statement. So instead of talking, they stare at each other or give a look of deep disappointment. Again, this was meant to be deceptive and not real.

The narcissistic mother believes she owes her child something that can't be paid back. So this means that the narcissistic mother made many sacrifices to have a daughter, putting her daughter in debt that she can never repay.

She wants her daughter to be moved by how much she gave up. If the sacrifice doesn't move the daughter, she is not grateful and, again, disappointed. So, we can see a clear theme through these signs.

Sign 7 — She Loves or Approves of Her Daughter When She Does What She Wants

This means that love or approval is not always present. It all depends on how well the daughter does.

I think some people would say that love that depends on performance is not love at all. If the daughter has to win or gain something through her performance, such as approval or love, is that the same as love?

Sign 8 — She Doesn't Respect Her Daughter's Boundaries

This includes searching her daughter's room, listening in on her conversations, reading her diary, and giving her daughter little privacy and a lot of criticism, partly based on what the mother finds out about privacy violations.

Another part of this would be to tell other people how bad the daughter is. Again, this is a boundary violation, so putting the daughter down in front of other people is a big parenting rule. It doesn't help a good relationship and can lead to many bad things.

Generally, daughters tend to trust their mothers and believe what they say; they think their parents know what to do, that everything they say is true, that they have the best ideas and that they know what they're doing, even though there isn't always proof to back this up. Parents don't have to be smart, reasonable, or logical to have children.

What Can a Daughter Do if Her Mother Is Narcissistic?

The only real advice that can be offered is to talk to a counselor. Someone has to figure out what's real and what's not in their relationship with their mother to help them believe that their feelings are real and admit their mother may not have done anything wrong.

However, regardless, their mother still let them down in the worst way possible by making them think everything was their fault.

Another question I'm often asked is whether or not the relationship should end? Should the narcissistic mother's daughter stop talking to her? This is a very hard choice to make.

As with most things, I think it would be best to talk to a counselor about this. On the other hand, biologically, a person can only have one mother, and ending a relationship differs from stopping all contact. I don't think they are the same, even though they may look the same.

I'm not sure that a mother-daughter relationship or any other parent-child relationship can end just because the child doesn't talk to the parent. People think one person can end a relationship, but there is more than one way to do this.

In a way, deciding not to talk to anyone is a choice. But just because you haven't talked to each other in a while doesn't mean the relationship is over. It won't be over until someone can make peace with it.

Therefore, you could say that the relationship is over. No one can talk to or contact that person, but the effect does not stop. The effects of a mother-daughter relationship can last even after they are no longer together.

I've seen this happen so often that I know it's hard for a daughter to find peace with the situation. even though the mother is no longer there, the feelings are as painful as when the mother was alive. People can't run away from or ignore their mother-daughter relationships because they don't get better over time.

Chapter 2:
Why Is She Like This?

I n this chapter, I will discuss the mental state of a narcissistic parent who abuses their child, for you, the reader, get to know the "enemy" or to figure out what type of person the parent was for them to consider their child to be a threat to their fragile sense of self-worth, and why they went out of their way to make their child feel worse than they did.

There are valid explanations for this type of behavior, particularly if we take the notion of narcissistic psychology seriously as an explanatory framework.

The Psychology of a Narcissist

The psychology of a narcissist begins with the narcissist's deep-seated belief that they are worth little. The narcissist's feelings will be harmed if forced to accept this; therefore, they use **antidotal tactics** (I call them antidotal since they do not fix the problem due to the narcissist's refusal to recognize the reality of the situation). They put off the consequences and burden the people around them by doing so.

The first aspect of an **antidotal tactic** is for the narcissist to flatly deny they feel worthless and insist the opposite–that they are more important, more special, or just plain better than others. That they are full of worth is what they consciously need to tell themselves. The terminology for this psychological train of thought is a **grandiose sense of self.**

The other part of the antidotal solution is the expectation that others are going to comply with their inflated view of themselves. The term for this is **entitlement.** Therefore, the narcissist will often act coercively towards others, whether implicitly or explicitly, to garner that reflection that they are as grandiosely good as they need to believe they are.

Now, these antidotes are just two aspects of their attempts to counter their feeling of worthlessness; they require significant self-absorption and a significant amount of self-aggrandizement or self-boosting.

It goes without saying, if a narcissistic mother is focused on herself and likes to boast or consider herself to be better than others, she will not have many friends. Therefore, the narcissist needs to guard others against this fact from becoming widely known.

What Happens When a Narcissist Has a Child?

Given these two features, it is not a far stretch for us to consider what happens when this type of person has a child and what they feel about themselves when they do.

During pregnancy, the narcissistic mother-to-be may believe their child will convey a further compliment to who they are. But what happens after birth when the child is, inevitably, a bundle of needs?

Simply put, the child will require an adult who loves them to meet those needs benignly, supportively, and lovingly.

A narcissist, however, is not motivated by support, kindness or love; their sense of worthlessness prevents them from cultivating these feelings towards their child, or anyone for that matter, and particularly, towards themselves.

Instead, what happens is that the narcissist must always be engaged to maintain their inflated self-sense. The interruptions associated with having a child are not taken kindly by the narcissist. When the antidotal processes are interrupted, the narcissist's sense of worthlessness grows.

For example, if a mother is extremely narcissistic, whenever she hears her baby crying because it wants to be fed, she might believe that the child thinks their needs are more important than hers.

That makes the narcissist feel more worthless; therefore, they take out their negativity on the child! In their mind, it is the child's fault if this reveals anything bad about them.

The child faces this terrible dilemma that their important needs constitute a psychological threat to the narcissistic mother and to her tenuous efforts to maintain her inflated self-esteem.

Consequences To Disrupting the Narcissistic Self-absorbing Processes

So, what happens when that inevitable disruption in the parent's self-absorbing processes occurs? The narcissistic mother has to restore their ability to focus on themselves. They do that in a very unfortunate way.

Initially, the narcissistic parent will often perceive the child as selfish: it is the child's fault that they are interrupting the narcissist's antidotal processes. The child, as far as the narcissist is concerned, does not think of others and is too needy.

Secondly, the narcissist will often try to manifest their sense of worthlessness within that child so they can diminish the child's esteem. If they know the child considers themselves worthless as the child grows older, that allows the narcissist a reprieve from the very same worthlessness they themselves experience. It is a process called **projective identification**.

Projective Identification

When a narcissist cannot bear a feeling, they coerce another person to experience the very same feelings. Then, the narcissist will maintain these feelings in that other person to experience relief or reprieve.

This means they must continually domineer the other person to ensure they are the bearer of the feelings the narcissist cannot stand.

For example, in the movie "**This boy's life,**" starring Robert DeNiro, his character finds fairly innocuous things in his stepson, portrayed by Leo DiCaprio, that become distorted reasons why DiCaprio's character is so selfish and why he's worthless. DeNiro, in this case, attempts to get DiCaprio to consider himself worthless in a way that DeNiro does not want to acknowledge and deflect his selfishness. I highly recommend the movie if you have time and interest in checking out the film to see how the movie illustrates this process of narcissistic blaming.

Chapter 3:
How Far Has Her Narcissism Affected Me?

I n this chapter, I'll talk about how a narcissistic mother's lack of emotional care affects you as an adult. I'll also detail what it means to have a narcissistic mother. I'll also talk about what happens when you live with someone who is supposed to care for you, pull you in, be your confidant, and have your back.

A mother is supposed to protect their child from the bad things and troubles of the world; however, when you have a narcissistic mother, the person you are most afraid of is the one who lives with you—the person you love, the person that, emotionally, psychologically, and even subconsciously, your entire being has been born to love and to need and to crave; therefore, there are grave consequences when you have a parent, specifically a mother, this hurt you as a child.

So, when you have a narcissistic mother, you have an unstable mother who could have anger issues, who might be highly critical of you, and, potentially, a very defensive mother. You have a mother who cannot see herself, who is shrouded in entitlement, and this entitlement shows up in many different ways.

The Three Themes of Growing up With a Narcissistic Mother

Daughters whose mothers are narcissists who have shared their experiences can identify **three themes** to describe growing up with a narcissistic mother.

Theme 1 — Power and Shame

The daughter is never appreciated by her mother; never once did anyone thank her nor did she have anyone help her or cheer her on. Because of this, she had to give up one of her most important goals: getting an education. The mother could not make a mistake, but the daughter could only do wrong.

The things the daughter chose to do or value were dismissed or put down as "silly," "worthless," and "not productive." If she chose something that met her mother's needs, that would be accepted, but most of the time, nothing her daughter did would meet her mother's approval.

The daughter's hopes and wishes would not be allowed, and she will start to consider herself to be her mother's extension. I've seen this happen many times in my work as a therapist.

This is how someone feels about a situation: the mother would always start fights because she knew she might win. This is interesting to me because it shows how the narcissist creates the situation on the battlefield.

They choose where they fight, when they fight, and under what conditions they fight. This gives them a market advantage when it comes to winning these arguments.

Power

The mother decides what is allowed and whether or not the daughter will do what she says. The daughter can't win here because she ends up in the same place either way she goes. Therefore, the daughter is stuck in this situation.

There aren't many things the narcissist can change about her daughter. Therefore, the daughter may be shamed in front of other people by her mother who can't control what she does.

The mother wasn't able to set good limits, and she did strange things. This shows that there was no safe place to turn in these situations. Once more, the daughter was stuck. The mother is not stable or reliable; therefore, the daughter never knows what to expect.

I've seen this idea of someone not being receptive to what their mother enjoyed a lot in my work as a therapist. People believe that they will fight back when their preferences are forced on them, which seems like a natural reaction. Therefore, the narcissist blames their children and everyone for how their life turned out.

Shame

This is believed to be the result of the nullification and the demonstration of power. Shame is when the daughter feels bad about herself because they can't do anything. This belief manifests itself as worthless. They base their sense of self on inferiority, worthlessness, ineffectiveness, and being flawed.

Theme 2 — For Children Who Grew up Alone

This behavior comprises four parts: being dependent, blaming, being jealous, and putting on a positive front.

Dependency

Starting with what is needed, the mother ensured that her daughter needed her. She kept her daughter from talking to other people, even friends because she saw other people as competition, and she didn't want the competition. The daughter's job was to meet her mother's needs. All the energy and attention in the house was drawn to the mother like a black hole.

It's hard to understand someone acts to get attention out of your mind. The mother might even attempt to pit her daughter against her husband. The daughter won't be allowed to date the boy she likes, and the daughter can't tell anyone about how much control there is. A big part of this dynamic is that the mother kept things secret.

Blaming

The mother can blame the daughter for anything without any reason. I've seen this often happen, where the child who grew up with a narcissistic parent never learned to trust that parent. They didn't know if the parent was telling the truth or trying to get them to do something. They never really settled down and felt safe.

So, this brings me to the third and fourth parts of growing up alone:

Jealously and Putting on a Positive Front

The mother hates other people to raise her damaged esteem. If the daughter compliments her behavior, the mother takes credit for it right away. While this might make the mother seem caring and sensitive in the eyes of her daughter, the harsh reality is very different.

Hose down the perfect image of the mother that other people have, and the daughter can't be happy unless it has something to do with her mother. Similarly, she can't be happy unless that happiness makes the mother look better or happy.

The tragic reality of the daughter's situation is that, being an only child, the daughter has nowhere to go on her own. The daughter can't do anything. This adds to the story of abuse because the daughter can't even talk to other people. As a result, no one will feel sorry for her. Even when someone is trapped, however, the daughter can take comfort in the fact that there could be the possibility that others can see them and understand how bad their situation is. This, however, is something the daughter is denied.

This brings me to the last theme:

Theme 3 — Denied a Childhood

This theme consists of three parts: violence and threats, and rejection.

Violence and Threats

When the mother wants to punish the daughter, she often hits her. There is no motivation. There are threats, and the daughter is always afraid of making her mom mad. The daughter learned that she should be careful of what she says and does.

The mother doesn't just hurt the daughter, however. The daughter needs to work; she has to work hard constantly to keep her mother happy. Therefore, the daughter remains in a constant state of terror and fear.

Rejection

The mother has never felt that her daughter was safe. The mother forgets about her, ignores her, and leaves her alone. She doesn't protect her, which sometimes lets other people treat her daughter badly. Therefore, the daughter worries about her mother and her mother's lack of protection. This presents opportunities for other people to try to hurt the daughter.

Most of the time, mothers look out for their daughters. The narcissistic mother, however, doesn't do this. Therefore, the mother is just being mean. She doesn't feel she is, so she doesn't care. Everything is about her.

What Results Would These Three Themes Lead To?

The answer is shame. In general, a childhood spent being reminded of being bad at things leads to feelings of inferiority and worthlessness. This makes the daughter hate everyone else and turn her attention to her mother.

Hypervigilance is another result of this because the absence of a healthy childhood leads to feelings of insecurity and fear. In general, people who are narcissistic mothers and their daughters are more likely to possess or develop insecure attachments, which makes them more likely to develop psychopathology.

This is all part of the path to mental illness. In this case, it is caused by an insecure attachment. While this is not the sole reason, it is a notable contributor. These daughters have a hard time telling others of their mother's narcissism because they don't know if anyone will listen to them or know how to help them.

The daughter's mother continually attempts to make the daughter feel isolated, even as she gets older.

The Two Trees Analogy

When I think of the mother-daughter dynamic (and this could be said about many dynamics), I think of two trees. One tree is a mother. The smaller tree is the daughter. As the daughter tree grows up, it is expected that it will grow straight and strong so that when the wind blows, it won't bend too much.

What we see here with these two trees, however, is that the mother is pulling the smaller tree either into her as that tree grows, or it pushes it away from her.

Either way, that tree does not end up straight; rather, it ends up curved to one side or the other. We know that it's not easy to separate two entangled trees. This is a very hard dynamic to change.

If, so to speak, the daughter tree is bent, that curve will be hard to straighten out. If the tree is separated, it might not necessarily be better for it because either the daughter tree is too close to the mother or too far away. Either way, the daughter tree's spine is curved unhealthy.

This is how I consider many situations between parents and children. People sometimes tell the children of narcissists, "Why don't you just stand up straight, like a tree?"

This isn't possible because there is a distortion that isn't easy to fix, and real life doesn't resemble the curve of a tree. Instead, it's more like a mistake in the way you think, which is something that counseling can help with.

Issues a Daughter Will Experience Being Raised by a Narcissistic Mother

Trust Issues

The first issue that we are going to talk about is trust issues. If you have had a narcissistic mother, you will likely experience trust issues because the person who was supposed to look out for you and love you did not show up for you.

Also, because how she appears to others is very different from how she is to you, you will see that a narcissist knows when they can act appropriately and when it is safe to act inappropriately.

So, a narcissistic mother will go into a rage towards her children when no one is around but wouldn't dare exhibit this behavior in front of her husband or around a neighbor or a co-worker because she wants to maintain that false persona.

Therefore, you are likely going to develop trust issues because you are not going to be able to trust the people who say they love you.

After all, your mother was your first role model for love and relationships, and she failed you and taught you that love was unsafe. From her, you learned that people are unreliable, so why even bother giving your trust away?

If you know that people, in general, are untrustworthy, will not show up for you, and make you feel worthless, why would you want to put your trust in them?

Being a Loner/Lone Wolf

You may identify with the concept of being a **lone wolf**. When you have a mother with narcissistic traits or who has narcissistic personality disorder or is a narcissist, you get the sense that not only can you trust this person, but it is not safe to need anyone; it is not safe to ask for help.

If you asked for help as a child, you got the impression that you were a burden to your narcissistic mother. You were a bother and perhaps got the sense that the best way to get your mother's love was to leave her alone, to stay in the darkness and ache for her love and hope that some way somehow you would be able to figure out how to be good enough to gain her love.

This manifests later on in life by taking on way too much. You end up not paying attention to it. When you are overwhelmed, you work yourself to your detriment without asking for help. You do not feel worthy of support. You believe asking for help symbolizes weakness, and you struggle with anyone ever perceiving you as a burden because it triggers the shame you felt as a child.

Poor Self-care

How do you know that you are worthy of self-care, except that the people who are supposed to love you infuse you with the idea that you are not worthy of self-care?

When we have narcissistic mothers who neglect us in terms of our emotions and our thinking, we are being ignored; our mothers are indifferent to us then. We believe we are not valuable, so why would we take care of some aspect of ourselves.

What if you've never gotten the impression or the message that the self is valuable? People usually tend to take better care of things that they think are valuable, but when we have no assigned value to it, it is not simple and easy to take care of the self and put the self first.

Narcissistic mothers do a wonderful job of infusing their children with the idea that they are not good enough, and those of us on this journey struggle with the "I am not enough" wound.

Fear of Losing Control

Another way you respond to being neglected by a narcissistic mother is that you fear losing control. The fear of losing control might be because your emotions feel as out of control as a child's. It could be because your mother was so out of control and you constantly looked for a way to feel in control.

So, what did you, as a child, do to tone yourself down? If mom is super upset, if she is excitable, if she is not calming down, if she is raging, and if she is criticizing us or she is treating us with indifference, this causes us to feel very emotionally destabilized.

You do not feel safe if your mother is not safe; if the mom is not grounded, you cannot feel grounded as a child.

Therefore, as a child, you tried to control yourself and ended up pushing down your emotions and pretending you were okay.

If you had a narcissistic mother, I encourage you to look back and see if you have any of these issues. Can you relate it to feeling so out of control as a child, and your need for control today as an adult is such that you think it has anything to do with being raised by someone whom you felt was out of control?

As a result of this, you attempt to control other people's emotions and what people do. Therefore, see if you can tie this back to feeling out of control as a child because how we respond to external stimuli shapes our personality and temperament, which ends up becoming a personality over time.

Suppression of Emotions

As a child, I associated pain with the feeling of being out of control; therefore, I developed coping strategies that helped me feel in power to suppress my emotions.

Although that might have made my mom happy, I might still be doing it subconsciously and not realizing it is comforting me at some level.

Although it is maladaptive, a part of me is growing towards a more successful mindset and staying on the personal development path despite having these situations with the narcissistic mother; therefore, I will be able to break through those patterns of belief that kept me stuck for so long.

Attraction to Those With High Narcissistic Traits

Some people believe this is our attempt to finish unfinished business from childhood. There was someone we loved that we were supposed to bond to that we never achieved that milestone; therefore, in our adult life, we might be taught in a cycle of repetition. We might be caught in the process of repetition compulsion.

You might be seen in a cycle of trying to get this unmet need in childhood met in adulthood. Although it would be subconscious, because you are not going to be attracted to someone who treated you like your parent did if your parent was a narcissist, you would subconsciously because you have these unmet wounds.

You are giving off specific energy, and, as we know, in the quantity field, like attracts like.

For example, although I might be more co-dependent, for instance, I might fear abandonment. Believe it or not, because of this, I am going to be attracted to someone who triggers that fear of abandonment because it is what I know until I get enough awareness around the situation and I can break through the patterns of beliefs and even the neurological pathways that are keeping me stuck at the subconscious level.

Therefore, you might feel attracted to narcissists subconsciously, and you might find yourself rationalizing why you are attracted to this person even though other people are telling you this guy is not good for you or this woman is not good for you.

You Seek Approval

On a subconscious level, however, you do not feel good enough and seek validation from the external world. This is because you never got the healthy mirroring you needed as a child, and subconsciously, you are still seeking a sense of validation from the outer world. Your mind is still stuck in that loop that "I am not good enough," and you need other people to tell you "I am good enough."

That's not true, but when you're stuck in a subconscious loop, you don't know that. That's why I keep bringing up the idea that to heal from codependency; you have to heal from the effects of being raised by a narcissistic mother.

This is as much a subconscious and neurological journey as an emotional, psychological, or spiritual journey. Been affected at the subconscious levels. Our brains have been wired to seek approval. We usually do not know if we are doing anything wrong.

If you are co-dependent, you come into a relationship looking to want to attach, and rationale goes out the window. If this person clicks all the boxes for you energetically and you feel attracted to this person, they could be pushing you away and moving you away.

All that is going to do is make you want this person more. Even if this person is a narcissist, you might be stuck seeking their approval because you never got the reapproval that you needed and deserve to develop a healthy sense of self when you were a child. This is because a narcissistic mother was raising you.

Fear of Having Children

This is more prevalent among females who have had narcissistic mothers. On a subconscious level (and occasionally a conscious level), we are afraid to have children because our mother was a narcissist, and we do not want to put our children through what our mother put us through.

The likelihood of you becoming a narcissistic mother is unlikely if you are already building empathy for a child you haven't yet had. However, this is a secret worry that many women who have had narcissistic mothers conceal.

They do not talk about them because they do not even know that is why they do not want children. Not every woman who decides that she does not have children is making that decision because she has a narcissistic mother, however.

We live in an age where women feel they have far more choices and control over their bodies or should have more control over themselves. Therefore, we have some work to do in that area, especially in other countries.

However, we live in a time when women feel more in control over their destinies and question whether or not they want to have children; not all women have those questions because of choice; rather, they are just exploring their options as modern women. Some of us who have had narcissistic mothers question whether we should have children because of our narcissistic parent(s).

Lack of Self-confidence

Let's talk about lack of self-confidence. Where does it stem from? Speaking for myself (to use myself as an example), it originates from what my parents, especially my mother, think about me, and I believe the being that created my personality.

My mother, the actual physical vehicle, the divine creation that created my divine creation, is the person that was my first experience with love.

So, if this person rejects you, how will you feel like you are worthy of love? If you do not feel you can trust the being who gave birth to you, how do you develop trust that you have something to offer the world and that other people should respect you?

If you are struggling with all these issues and were raised by a narcissistic mother, what I'd like you to take away from this chapter is that it is not your fault that everything you feel is normal. It is what happens when children feel rejected by the being supposed to love them, protect them, and nurture them.

You are not crazy, and you are not off, and even if the people in your outer world do not get it, you have to know that this is a real thing, that narcissistic mothers exist, and the consequences of being raised by someone whom you are supposed to love and trust and cannot love and trust are vast, and they are real.

It does not mean that you are broken. It just means that we have to get you to turn the ship around and start paying attention to the self and loving yourself the way your mother was supposed to love you, and if you can do that, you can create great success in your life despite the past.

Chapter 4:
Narcissistic Triangulation

N arcissists employ a variety of tactics to maintain control over their victims and keep them trapped in a vicious cycle. Narcissists manipulate their victims through a variety of underhanded methods, including **narcissistic triangulation**.

Why do narcissists engage in triangle-drawing? This chapter will provide an in-depth analysis of the impact of narcissistic triangulation on the victim in various settings and contexts.

What is Narcissistic Triangulation?

From a narcissistic perspective, narcissistic triangulation is one of several tactics used to inflict pain on their victims. So what exactly is meant by the term "narcissistic triangulation?"

This entails bringing a third person into the relationship who is either unknown or not very well known. Even if the third person is not necessarily the narcissist's victim, they are nonetheless included in the triangulation.

The tactic "divide and conquer" is another name for the narcissistic triangulation approach.

Why Does a Narcissist Engage in Triangulation?

Narcissists use you and another person as a triangle to get what they want. What a narcissist wants is:

- To assume the role of leader;

- To urge you to chase them;

- To cause you to feel uneasy;

- To introduce a state of anarchy.

Consequently, the narcissistic supply, consisting of a sense of entitlement and superiority, is successfully revived.

How Do Narcissists Triangulate Their Relationships?

The third person in the triangle will find it hard or impossible to talk to the narcissist. The narcissist keeps their distance out of caution so that they will not be found and so that they may more easily exert their influence over you.

When the third person tries to speak with the third person in the narcissistic triangle, the narcissist becomes upset and begins to abuse you verbally.

Triangulation strategies are used by narcissists to perpetrate abusive behaviors toward their partners, such as manipulation, love bombing, ghosting, and gaslighting. These behaviors are played out at the victim's expense in the relationship.

The narcissist will use different triangulation methods on their victim as the victim's circumstances shift. They use various techniques to extract various narcissistic resources from the connection at hand, whether it be a narcissistic love, a narcissistic family, a narcissistic employment, or a narcissistic friendship.

Let's take a look at some specific instances of how narcissists apply the strategy of triangulation to a variety of different sequences.

The Different Triangulation Strategies

As previously said, narcissists adapt their strategies for narcissistic triangulation to fit their particular circumstances. Narcissists consider the triangulation strategy a significant theatrical stage and tend to act on it exactly how they want when using it. The triangulation allows them to exercise control over either or both victims.

How they abuse and manipulate the victim also differs according to the situation's specifics.

Let's look at a few scenarios. For each, I'll provide an example of how they triangulate the victim.

Familial Triangulation

Triangulation in narcissistic families has been described as, "deceiving, manipulative," and can potentially split families.

It is entirely conceivable for one or both of the parents in a narcissistic family to also exhibit narcissistic tendencies. It can be challenging to grow up with a narcissistic parent when you realize that all of their care and concern is directed toward achieving their own selfish goals and that this is followed by narcissistic abuse.

However, now that you have suffered sufficient suffering, you are mature enough to know their true character. That is because they reared you without ever having heard of narcissism.

Within a narcissistic family, your sibling, a parent, a relative, or even a friend could play the role of your triangulation partner.

In **familial triangulation**, you are familiar with the other person involved but do not get along with them for some reason. The narcissist in your family will trick you into believing they can help you solve your problems and act as a mediator between you and your partner.

According to the findings of psychologists, the narcissists involved in the triangle may form relationships with one victim while inflicting harm on another.

It will appear as though the problem has been handled with the assistance of the narcissist, but in reality, it will not be. You and the other person are going to start arguing with each other once more. It will seem like you are on a rollercoaster as the tensions build up and are simultaneously resolved.

Even when the narcissist appears to be a supporter, you will not comprehend the fundamental cause of those dramas until you completely comprehend the issue. This is true even if the narcissist is trying to help you.

Narcissists can alter the meaning of your words, actions, or other behaviors to produce conflict between you and the other triangle members. This conflict can be caused by your words, acts, or behaviors.

Even something as simple as giving someone a look could be used as evidence against you if the other person interprets it as meaning something specific.

Narcissistic Triangulation Within the Family

An example of the narcissistic triangulation that can occur inside a family. Assume that the family members of the narcissistic single mother, who was the subject of the triangulation, were the son and daughters. If the children were younger, the narcissistic triangulation would consist primarily of a prejudiced comparison of one child over the other.

As a consequence, the children develop feelings of pessimism and insecurity. Let's use the son as an example; any child has the potential to become the narcissistic mother's favorite, and she may place an unhealthy amount of emphasis on him.

On the other hand, while her son receives praise and admiration, her daughter will be subjected to humiliation, guilt, abuse, gaslighting, and other similar behaviors. The son who receives excessive affirmation from his mother may develop narcissistic tendencies.

If the victims were adults, the narcissistic triangulation might take a different form and be more challenging. For example, while acting as if she is the children's carver, a narcissistic mother could try to pit her two children against one another to garner more attention. She can present herself as the victim in the triangle by using terms like these, which are part of the triangulation:

- "A family should never be separated from one another";

- "Allow me to have a conversation with him on your behalf";

- "My very own daughter was the one who was critical of me";

- "My passing away is the one thing that can permanently link the two of you together";

- The speaker offered a prayer, asking God to "take me and unite this family";

- "If I am not around, the two of you are going to kill each other with your fists";

- "I have been working on this to maintain our family's integrity."

Narcissists will always talk about themselves in everything they say. Children are going to believe this story about the victims and are under the impression that their narcissistic mother cares about them.

The narcissist is the primary factor responsible for all those siblings' problems.

The Most Effective Method for Dealing With Narcissistic Triangulation

Removing a narcissist from the situation might be difficult when involved in a narcissistic triangle. It is possible that the other person or people in your close area respect and believe in them, especially given how credible they are.

As a result, getting rid of them prematurely could make you appear less trustworthy from the perspective of other people.

Therefore, use these powerful tactics to remove the narcissist from the triangle:

1. Make an effort to dismiss the allegation made by the narcissists;

2. Determine what their intentions are;

3. Try not to show any signs of emotion;

4. Give the highest emphasis to other trustworthy people;

5. Do not show any emotion in your response (Gray-Rock Method);

6. Reduce the amount of time spent communicating;

7. Ensure that you make direct eye contact with the other person participating in the triangulation;

8. Define your parameters; and

9. If you absolutely must, try to avoid physical contact.

The first thing I would like you to do when it comes to triangulation is to be realistic. You want to stay as realistic as possible. People who engage in triangulation also have a skewed perception of reality.

They cannot dissect things appropriately, and they cannot process and reason maturely, partly because they go to a third person to create that triangle. They find those who are going to want to be a rescuer, or somebody they know is going to persecute the person you know they want to persecute; therefore, a lot of the time, it is going to be central for you to be as realistic as possible.

Keep Facts in the Forefront and Be as Objective as Possible

Consult with somebody objective, not very emotional, subjective, and opinionated. You want to stay as objective and factual as possible and realistic with a person who triangulates.

Look for parts of a story or conversation where there are many inconsistencies and things are not making sense.

Ask why she would say that and why he would do that; so you want to question things and pick and pull apart those inconsistencies.

Somebody who engages in triangulation also engages in pathological lying.

When you notice inconsistencies, you want to be able to point them out and say, "No, that does not make sense," or, "Wait a minute, that is not what you said last time." Be smart and get to the bottom of what's happening. You want to pull the facade apart; you want to break through the cobwebs, and you want to reach the heart of the matter. Many times that involves looking for inconsistencies because somebody who triangulates will display inconsistencies, just you watch.

Seek Proof

The whole idea of becoming a Columbo-like detective is unnecessary; simple investigatory skills are enough to catch the person who is being inconsistent or is lying.

You do not need to make it look like you are trying to catch them, of course, but you want to always be focused on the facts and objective parts of a situation when it comes to somebody who triangulates.

They are typically immature; they do not know how to switch their emotions, and they engage in lying behavior when they believe they are not accountable.

They do not engage in logical reasoning, and they are very opinionated, so you want to be able to look at the facts and the objectivity, that is, the situation and proof of what is true and what is not.

I know it is going to be very difficult, but you want to look for the truth if you want to look for proof and stay with the facts.

Report Abuse

Let's say you have identified somebody who's triangulating and they are also engaging in perennial parental alienation, or they are exhibiting authoritarian attitudes through their parenting, e.g., they were very harsh, stern, unfair, etc. In that case, you want to report that abuse.

The first place to report that abuse is to a layman or somebody who does not have credentials (such as a mandated reporter or even just a neighbor or a cousin). Then, reach out to the Child Protective Services Agency and tell them that you'd like to report abuse.

If you do not have a clear understanding as to whether or not it is abuse, then say, "Is there anybody that I can speak to? I have a hypothetical situation and I want to know that, if this were happening, should I be reporting it?"

That might be helpful as it will allow you to communicate with someone who understands the system and will allow you to talk to them about your issue without dropping names and personal information.

 It also allows you to ascertain if what you are describing does indeed need to be reported, and you can call Child Protective Services to do that.

Go To Counseling

Consider this option if parental alienation or triangulation is happening and the person is being manipulative or pathologically unstable (or lying pathologically). This is not because you need it, but because you need to know how to deal with the person driving you crazy.

Educating yourself on how to deal with the triangulating person would be best. This will allow you to break out of the narcissistic triangle and start living in peace with other people.

In addition, if you follow these guidelines, there is a possibility that narcissists will eventually stop trying to interact with you because they believe you are aware of their tactics.

To summarize, narcissists treat triangulation as if it were a game. They have complete power over the situation within the triangle as long as you do not figure out what they are. Because of this, narcissistic triangulation is bad for your relationships, including those in your family, at work, and even with your friends. It could also be difficult to stay away from other people.

However, establishing boundaries and improving your sense of self-worth can reduce the likelihood of becoming trapped in a triangulation and speed up the process of escaping narcissistic abuse.

Chapter 5:
A Narcissistic Mother's Strategies for Adult Daughters

A narcissistic mother will exploit her children as pawns in her power struggle for as long as they are alive, which might be their entire lives. She will experiment with various methods to confound and control her offspring like the other people in her life. Whenever they do something that makes her unhappy, she will behave harshly and will act cruelly toward them, emotionally.

When children become adults, they continue to use the manipulative methods they learned as children. In later years, a narcissistic mother is more likely to utilize methods typically employed toward their adult daughters.

These strategies can include controlling, coercive, and exploitative behavior. Her ways of getting people to do what she wants are not as obvious as they seem because she feels the need to conceal the fact that she wants to control people.

Even when you are an adult, it is likely your narcissistic mother will still try to control you.

As was covered in the previous chapter, the narcissistic mother will use the tactic of triangulation in her relationships to make them more complicated.

When a narcissist uses triangulation, they bring three sides together to meet in the middle. It is a move that is par for the course for a mother who's only concerned with herself. She begins utilizing it when her children are young and continues to do so even after they have grown up.

She may tell you one thing and your spouse something quite different, just like she did when you were a child.

Trust and communication may break down in your relationships as a direct result of what your egocentric mother demands.

She would much rather have your trust placed solely in her than in anyone else. She may build a case against you using information from your coworkers, friends, and family that may prevent you from advancing in your career, and may be the reason you lost your current position.

Nagging Mothers

Nagging mothers who are also narcissists are the worst nags out there. They will frequently unceasingly bother you until you give in to their demands.

They will never stop criticizing your actions, from the things you wear to the places you frequently go to the individuals you hang out with. They want to dictate your every action and have you completely rely on their judgment at all times.

Your narcissistic mother will have the hope that you will constantly feel compelled to tell her about the plans you have for the future. They want to have input on all of the meaningful choices you make.

To put it another way, they are ready to badger you into submission if it becomes necessary. The never-ending criticism your narcissistic mother leveled at you when you were little did not stop, and it will not stop now. You are an adult, and the complaints will continue until you ultimately learn to ignore them and move on with your life.

Your narcissistic mother will never stop looking for ways to criticize anything you do. She would like you to postpone making decisions until you have a chance to discuss them with her first. However, even if you gave in to her requirements, that wouldn't be enough. Even in those situations, she could find something to criticize.

It would benefit you to accept that she will never be content with you.

Constant Surveillance

A common symptom of narcissistic personality disorder in mothers is engaging in unlawful surveillance of their adult offspring.

Your narcissistic mother is likely to follow in the footsteps of other narcissistic mothers' habitual snooping. She will monitor your social media accounts and employ what she discovers about you to exercise power and authority over you.

Whenever she has some spare time, she will devote it to figuring out how to get into your phone. She will read your communication, regardless of how private it is, even if you send it to her.

A woman preoccupied with her needs will not let anyone, especially her children, have privacy. People in narcissists' lives have no right to privacy since the narcissist sees those people as extensions of herself and treats them as such.

You probably already know this because narcissistic mothers never talk about their children behind their children's backs; however, she does not think it is improper that she has been keeping an eye on you.

Negative Back-Talk

In addition, your narcissistic mother will talk about you negatively to other people. She will cause harm to your spouse, the people you work with, and your friends. She will extract whatever information she can from them and then use it against you.

You can never be sure whom she will tell about what you have said about a person, but she may tell your mutual friends whom she dislikes what you have said about them.

Imagine that she shared this with someone who might become a romantic interest. And if you tell her something extremely private, she may discuss it with other people, including those she works with or friends. Sometimes she'll spill the beans to gauge your reaction to the news.

She can cause significant damage by utilizing this method, and she will not think twice about employing it again if she believes doing so will benefit her interests.

Gaslighting

Gaslighting is best exemplified by a mother who is narcissistic and self-absorbed. Gaslighting is a common tactic utilized by narcissistic mothers and is also one of their favorite methods of manipulation.

This potentially lethal strategy is something that narcissists, in general, are experts in, but the narcissistic mother, in particular, is a master of it.

She will have accomplished her goal of getting you to question reality if she successfully makes you question your senses' reliability. She is certain that you will seek her guidance at some point. If this is the case, then you can be certain that her warped perspective will distort any explanation she provides. This is one more tactic she uses to win your dependence on her.

Holding Children to Unreasonable Standards

The worst kind of mothers are those who continually and unfairly hold each of their children to unreasonable standards.

This is just one more offensive and cruel strategy that your narcissistic mother will employ to knock your self-esteem to an all-time low and get you to grovel for her attention.

She will continually compare you and one another to one another, as well as your siblings, their friends, and the children of her friend's friends. No matter what you achieve, you will never be capable of competing on an equal level with anyone else.

She constantly compares you to others, which can strain even the most intimate friendships. She will present these comparisons to you in a manner that makes it difficult for you to refute them.

She will make it quite clear that you are not good enough by continuously drawing comparisons between you and others. This may have a significant impact on how you feel about yourself.

Immediate Demand For Results

Narcissism is characterized by an impatience for results and a demand to get them immediately. When you are in a bind, she'll be understanding and patient with you, but whenever she makes a request, she expects an immediate response from you.

If you do not instantly give in to her demands, she will begin to shame you. And then, once you have caved into her requirements, she'll be even more specific about what she needs from you. As soon as she no longer needs it, she will complain that it is insufficient or irrelevant.

She does not recognize the concept of an unjust request and always anticipates that you'll take care of whatever she needs right away. As a result, she will conclude that her needs are not a top priority, even if there is the tiniest delay in satisfying them.

Sense of Entitlement

In most cases, narcissistic mothers develop an overpowering sense of entitlement in their children. This frequently results in their children being dependent on them and putting their mother's requirements before their own.

For a narcissist, this is the ideal situation. When their children experience a moment they perceive to be significant, narcissistic mothers are either absent or arrive late to the event. It is just one more way of showing that they add more value to the collaboration than you do, which is the point of this strategy.

It is a more understated way to demonstrate that you are in charge of the situation. They are unable to gather the emotional strength to convey their gratitude for the actions they have taken.

Self-Reflection

Narcissistic mothers may see you as a reflection of themselves, but that does not guarantee they'll let you have your moment in the spotlight.

They are under the impression that if they do not show up on time or at all for an event that they consider significant, they are causing you pain and displaying how much influence they have over your lives. Mothers who are entirely focused on themselves rarely support their children.

Lack of Empathy

Your mother's narcissism will prevent her from being warm and compassionate. To be able to do it for the people who are important to them requires empathy, which narcissists typically lack. A narcissist cannot genuinely empathize with other people. They cannot imagine or even fathom what it would be like to be in your shoes. They are clueless about it.

Everyone is so focused on gratifying their wants and needs that they cannot think about anything else. It is possible to claim that this is their fundamental driving force.

To sustain oneself, an individual requires what psychotherapists refer to as a "narcissistic supply," which is a consistent flow of praise and approval. They depend on it to enhance their sense of self-worth, and as a result, they cannot function without it.

As a direct consequence of this, people have difficulty demonstrating empathy. They cannot self-soothe because they do not possess the emotionally stable identity necessary for doing so, and they cannot console others because they do not possess the necessary abilities. Because of this, your narcissistic mother could never make you feel truly comfortable in the face of the hard things that happened in your life, no matter how hard she tried.

One more point: a narcissistic mother is the antithesis of the image of a nurturing parent that most people have in their heads. She is neither kind nor supportive but rather harsh and narcissistic rather than loving and supportive.

Even when they are adults, she has no compunction about abusing her children with harsh techniques. You can only break free of her manipulations if you acknowledge them for what they are and begin to take responsibility for your own choices.

The first step to healing is coming to terms with the reasons behind your mother's self-centered behavior. Discover in the following chapters how this decision has altered the course of your life. Familiarity and knowledge of her personality will make it easier for you to comprehend your conduct.

Chapter 6:
What is PTSD? What is CPTSD? Why Should I Know About It?

P ost-traumatic stress disorder is a type of mental illness that some people develop after they've experienced something shocking, scary, or dangerous.

During and after a traumatic event, it is normal to feel scared. Fear makes the body do many things quickly to help protect itself against danger or to flee from it. This "fight-or-flight" reaction is common to keep a person safe.

Almost everyone reacts differently to trauma, but most get over the first symptoms alone. People who continue to have problems may be given a diagnosis of PTSD and might feel anxious or scared, even when not in danger.

Complex Post-Traumatic Stress Disorder (CPTSD)

The World Health Organization's new International Classification of Diseases (ICD-11) has a new category called complex post-traumatic stress disorder (CPTSD) (WHO).

A new study in The Lancet calls CPTSD "a severe mental disorder that develops in response to traumatic life events." CPTSD is post-traumatic stress disorder (PTSD). According to the study, this disorder affects between 1% and 8% of the general population, and up to 50% of people live in mental health facilities.

For the study, researchers from the University of Zurich made a list of the signs and symptoms of CPTSD. They found that CPTSD has "three core post-traumatic symptom clusters" and "chronic and pervasive disturbances in emotion regulation, identity, and relationships...

People with complex PTSD have usually been exposed to trauma for a long time or more than once, like abuse as a child or violence at home or in the community."

CPTSD vs. PTSD

PTSD is one of the most common ways of dealing with trauma. Experts have known for a long time, though, that some trauma victims or survivors show a wider pattern of mental changes.

Therefore, in 1988, Judith Herman, a professor of clinical psychology at Harvard, coined the term CPTSD to describe the consequences of long-term trauma. Some of the symptoms between PTSD and CPTSD are very similar, including flashbacks or feeling like that trauma is happening right now.

At least 29 studies from over 15 countries have shown that CPTSD and PTSD differ.

A 2018 Journal of Psychiatric Practice report says, "Complex PTSD, also called developmental PTSD, is a group of symptoms that can be caused by long-term, chronic exposure to traumatic experiences, especially in childhood. This is different from PTSD, which is usually caused by a single traumatic event or set of traumatic events."

CPTSD is not listed as a separate condition in the DSM-5 (Diagnostic and Statistical Manual of Mental Disorders).

The researchers wrote, "Even though it has been a controversial diagnosis and is not in the DSM-5, there is evidence to support its unique profile and usefulness."

According to the updated ICD-11, a clinician must decide that a person meets all the criteria for traditional PTSD and shows problems with self-regulation, low self-esteem, a sense of shame or guilt related to past trauma, and trouble keeping relationships with others before diagnosing complex trauma.

The updated ICD-11 also added self-organization disturbances to the list of PTSD symptoms. These include having too many or too strong emotional responses, feeling like you are not worth anything, and having trouble keeping relationships and feeling close to other people.

Do I Have PTSD Or CPTSD?

Most, but not all, people who have been traumatized have short-term symptoms, but most do not develop long-term (chronic) PTSD. Some people with PTSD have never been in a dangerous situation. PTSD can also be initiated by things like the sudden death of a loved one.

Most of the time, symptoms show up quickly, within three months of the traumatic event, but sometimes they appear years later. For someone to have PTSD, their symptoms must last for more than a month and be terrible enough to get in the way of relationships or work.

The illness can go in different directions. Some people feel better in 6 months, while others' symptoms last for a long time. Some people have had the condition for a long time.

PTSD can be diagnosed by a psychiatrist or psychologist who has helped people with mental illnesses.

An adult should have all of the following symptoms for at least one month for PTSD to be diagnosed:

- At least one symptom that comes back

- At least one avoidance symptom

- At least two indications of arousal and reactivity

- At least two mental and emotional signs

Symptoms that come back include:

- Flashbacks are repeated memories of the trauma,

- which can cause physical symptoms like a racing heart or sweating.

- Nightmares

- Thoughts that scare you

Re-experiencing symptoms can make it hard to go about daily life. The person's thoughts and feelings can lead to the first signs. Words, things, or situations that remind someone of the event can also cause symptoms to come back.

Avoidance symptoms include:

- Avoiding places, events, or things that bring back memories of the traumatic event

- Trying not to think or feel about the traumatic event

When someone has avoidance symptoms, things that remind them of the traumatic event can make them act out. Because of these symptoms, a person may have to change how they do things. For example, a person who usually drives may not drive or ride in a car again after a bad car accident.

- Some signs of arousal and reactivity are:

- Easily getting scared

- Feeling tense or "on edge."

- Having trouble falling asleep

- Having fits of anger

Most of the time, arousal symptoms are always there and are not brought on by things that remind a person of the distressing event. These symptoms can make a person feel angry and stressed out. They might make it hard to do everyday things like sleep, eat, or focus.

- Symptoms of thinking and feeling bad are:

- Having trouble remembering important parts of the scary event

- Thoughts that are bad about yourself or the world

- Distorted feelings like guilt or blame

- Loss of interest in fun things

After a traumatic event, thinking and feeling problems can start or get worse. These problems are not caused by injury or drug use. Instead, these symptoms can make someone feel like they do not belong with their friends or family.

After a dangerous event, it is normal to have one or two of these symptoms for a few weeks. PTSD may cause symptoms that last longer than a month, make it hard to do normal things, and are not caused by drugs, illness, or anything else but the event itself. Some people with PTSD go weeks or months without showing any signs. Depression, drug abuse, or one or more anxiety disorders often go hand in hand with PTSD.

Do Children and Adults Act Differently?

Children and teens can have very strong reactions to trauma, but some symptoms may differ from those of adults. Symptoms that are sometimes seen in children younger than six years old can include the following:

- Able to use the bathroom but still wetting the bed,

- Not being able to talk or forgetting how to speak,

- Reenacting the scary event as a game,

- Being overly attached to a parent or another adult.

Older kids and teens are more likely to have symptoms similar to adults. They may also act in annoying, disrespectful, or harmful ways. Older kids and teens may feel bad that they did not stop anyone from getting hurt or dying. They might also want to get back at you.

In Complex post-traumatic stress disorder, you have some of the symptoms of PTSD as well as some other symptoms, such as:

- Trouble keeping your feelings in check and controlling your emotions,

- Feeling terribly angry or suspicious of everyone and everything,

- Feeling empty or without hope all the time,

- Feeling like you are broken or worthless for good,

- Feeling like you are a different person from everyone else,

- Feeling like no one understands what's going on,

- Avoiding relationships and friendships or finding them very hard,

- Having dissociative symptoms like depersonalization and derealization a lot,

- Some physical signs are headaches, dizziness, chest pains, and stomach aches,

- Regular suicidal feelings.

If you have complex PTSD, you might experience what some call an "emotional flashback." This is when you have strong feelings like fear, shame, sadness, or despair that you felt during the trauma. You might act as if things happening in the present are making you feel this way, not realizing that you are having a flashback.

Why Does Complex PTSD Happen?

The following types of traumatic events can cause complex PTSD:

- Abuse, neglect, or being left alone as a child,

- Ongoing violence or abuse in the home,

- Seeing violence or abuse over and over,

- Forcing or tricking someone into prostitution (trading sex), torture, kidnapping, or slavery,

- Being a war prisoner.

Complex PTSD is more likely to happen to you if:

- You had a bad experience when you were young,

- It took eternities to get over the trauma,

- It was hard or impossible to escape or get help,

- You have been through a lot,

- Someone close to you hurt you in some way.

How to Diagnose Complex PTSD?

It is not as easy as one might think to determine if someone has CPTSD. Since it is a relatively new disorder, many doctors do not know much about it. In addition, it is often confused with PTSD or borderline personality disorder (BPD).

Getting a detailed diagnosis is an initial step to getting the right treatment. Once a person has been diagnosed, they can choose between in-patient and out-patient programs. Since there is no one test for CPTSD, patients must prepare for their appointment.

To help the doctor figure out what's wrong with them, patients should:

- Write down all the symptoms;

- Mark When Symptoms Started;

- Keep an eye on how the symptoms change;

- Write down how bad each symptom is;

- Find out what sets them off.

The doctor will probably ask about bad things that happened in the past. They will also ask about family history and health to determine other problems.

Being honest about medications, drugs, and alcohol is very important. This info can help the doctor make a treatment plan for you. Some people need two diagnoses and the treatments that go with them.

CPTSD and Narcissism

As we have seen, having narcissistic parents can hurt kids in many ways. But when C-PTSD is added, things get even worse. The trauma is made worse by narcissism.

On the one hand, the child will feel rejected as they grow up. Or, they, too, become narcissists who are sure they are better than everyone else and try to control, insult and push people away. Neither of them will have dealt with and healed from the things that happened to them as kids. So, they carry around the trauma that hasn't been dealt with. This, in turn, affects how they get along with adults throughout their lives.

Chapter 7:
Is She the Reason for My CPTSD?

I n this chapter, we will discuss how the narcissistic mother is linked to Complex Post-Traumatic Stress Disorder (CPTSD). In the previous chapter, we discussed PTSD, CPTSD, and their signs and symptoms in detail. Now, we will discuss the link between the narcissistic mother and CPTSD.

CPTSD is quite complicated. It is an intricate web of so many things, just like the narcissists cast their net, which you get caught in. And then you get caught in your web, even if you have gone no contact or cut off contact with a narcissistic mother.

When we think about **Post-Traumatic Stress Disorder** (PTSD), it refers to a condition that is a response to a single event characterized by symptoms such as flashbacks to the original trauma. Maybe it was a car accident, an experience of sexual assault, or about veterans or people who experience combat-related trauma.

Even though the left logical side of your brain understands that it is not occurring in the present, you still have memories of the experiences. As a result, you have intrusive thoughts, images, physical sensations, etc. This always occurs in the clients I work with, including sweating or night sweats, night terrors, re-living that experience, nausea, etc.; it is as if it is happening again right now as if you are re-living it.

The Causes of CPTSD

Not all children of narcissistic mothers will develop CPTSD, and people who have seen CPTSD also often experience emotional adjustment difficulties, feelings of emptiness and utter hopelessness, feelings of hostility, and feelings of distrust.

They feel like, inherently, at the core, they are broken, and something is wrong with them. They may well buy into the idea that there is something integrally defective. After all, the reasons for feeling sad, anxious, or hopeless have all been laughed at and denied by the person who set you up.

The causes of CPTSD are rooted in long-term trauma, the accumulation of trauma not just one event but the accumulation of many occasions over time, and it can be due to any ongoing trauma such as domestic abuse or living in a hostile environment.

However, it is most often associated with trauma that occurred in childhood, and those obvious childhood traumas could be physical and sexual abuse and emotional neglect.

Those physical experiences leave external scars, but internal imperfections, like those blind scars left by emotional neglect, leave the most severe significant impact. Emotional abuse is more difficult to identify than physical abuse. The signs are more clear with emotional abuse. There are cuts and bruises; you know you are going to the doctor immediately to receive treatment; however, for emotional abuse, you do not go to a doctor directly.

You are made to push it down, deal with it, or get over it. That can be much more difficult to identify. It also does not show up until later when you see this impact in your adult life. You are out of that experience that caused that, but it is still there. It is like a snowball; it keeps rolling, getting bigger and moving faster, causing more damage.

Emotional Abuse

Emotional abuse is at the heart of children who grow up with a narcissistic parent, specifically a narcissistic mother; the emotional abuse is disguised, and it is deeply hidden as bonds of love.

In an ideal world, you would have been allowed to grow up simply being a kid; you got the opportunity for freedom of self-exploration and self-expression. You were free to be curious, have dreams, and express yourself.

But in the world of a narcissistic parent or mother, all of that was squashed and diminished. It all became about serving and being controlled and manipulated to serve that parent or that mother, so children of narcissistic mothers do not get the luxury of having a childhood or being a kid.

Instead, they live a continuous state of fear, of walking on eggshells, although it is probably like walking on knives or blades.

It is almost as if this narcissistic mother set of rules you are expected to live by, and you feel like you never get it right; even if you do get it right the next time you go in, the rules are completely different and change.

Therefore, you feel trapped in a never-ending cycle of criticism and fear. Receiving this criticism is every bit as frightening to that child as getting slapped or physically punished for whatever it was that they did, and along with that fear is constant confusion.

Here are two examples of emotional abuse and its consequences.

Example 1

Let's say, for example, you have your grandmother, but you know that your mother is jealous of your grandmother for whatever reason.

Instead of being free to express your love to your grandmother because she treats you wonderfully and gives you true genuine love, you know that your mother is jealous of her.

As a result, instead of being allowed to express your love to her, you might find yourself thinking or saying nasty things about your grandmother, maybe even to please your mother.

Example 2

Here's another example, let's imagine that you are a naturally outgoing child, but because of your natural outgoing ability, your ability to connect with anyone and for others to like and love you, your mother quickly becomes jealous when you take that limelight or that spotlight away from her.

Therefore, simply expressing sadness or fear is met with mockery or with disdain, and she laughs at you by saying, "What are you crying about come on oh your life is so hard right."

As a result, the consequence of having an emotionally detached and unhealthy parent is fear of abandonment.

The Effects of Emotional Abuse

Trust Issues

Individuals with unhealthy parents grow up without learning how to trust other people, how to engage in relationships in a healthy way, and how to love and reciprocate love and affection.

As a result, you might also be likely to be afraid of people leaving you as you haven't been supported in your growth and were invalidated for so long. So why should they trust now?

Neediness Within Yourself

The next thing you'll likely see is neediness within yourself. This comes from that lack of validation and emotional and psychological support. Therefore, you want to find that somewhere else. These needs may lead you into bad relationships!

Violence and prostitution breed rape and molestation situations where your money, finances, and stability are jeopardized. Even sexual rendezvous and affairs can be the result of that neediness and your desire to try to fill that empty void that was created due to growing up under an unhealthy and detached parent.

Difficulty with Intimacy

Intimacy does not just refer to a physical connection. It can also refer to getting to know somebody at the core of who they are, having a closeness and a familiarity with them, and being able to manage your emotions with their emotions and your needs with their needs.

However, having an equal and balanced relationship without this knowledge in your life growing up under this unhealthy parent, you are likely to struggle in that area.

Let me explain how your brain acts in these situations. I call it **central nervous system dominance**.

Central Nervous System Dominance

We all have two systems. One is the **central nervous system**, and the other is the **peripheral nervous system**. The peripheral nervous system exists outside of our joints are bones. Our circular system exists outside the central nervous system.

The **central nervous system** consists of two main parts: the brain, and the spinal cord. The central nervous system is comprised of two different systems: the **sympathetic nervous system** and the **parasympathetic nervous system**.

The Sympathetic Nervous System

The sympathetic nervous system is like a gas pedal. The body speeds up when you feel like you are in danger.

When you see a threat, when post-traumatic stress disorder gets triggered by something, when you get upset, when you get anxious, when you have a panic attack, etc., your sympathetic nervous system kicks into the gas pedal mode, and your parasympathetic nervous system is the part of your body that I refer to. The brake system is like pumping the brakes. You are no longer anxious and no longer have an increased heart rate. You are no longer sweating and feeling like you need to battle, or run, or hide.

The Parasympathetic Nervous System

The parasympathetic nervous system is that part of your body. That system says, "everything will be okay, and I will calm down."

When you have been raised in an unhealthy and toxic environment, your body becomes conditioned to being in the sympathetic nervous system gas pedal mode, and that fight or flight mode gets kicked off when it really should not. And so you may be in that mode when you should not be.

As a result, your body is constantly in overdrive, and you are continually filling up, anxious, panicky, nervous, and unstable. That is the physiological and neurological consequence of growing up in a household like this.

Understanding The Amygdala

Here comes another brain structure known as **the amygdala**. The amygdala is an important part of the brain. It is like an almond size structure in the middle of the brain. What happens in the amygdala?

The amygdala is not logical. It has no intellect and does not know how to decipher between two things. It is like a flashlight looking for threats that might harm a person.

It explores your environment to see if there is any danger, and if it senses something that might be threatening, it goes haywire. The process creates strong emotions, like fear, pleasure, or anger. It also sends signals/messages to the cerebral cortex, which controls conscious thought.

Signals from the thalamus to the autonomic nervous system and skeletal muscles control physical reactions and increase your heart rate. This results in your mind racing, panicking, or sweating. Your body enters fight or flight mode or gas pedal mode.

Because of the damage to the amygdala, narcissists are stuck in a constant state of fear and anxiety. They also have bad reactions to things in the environment that remind them of violations to themselves. This means that narcissists are always on guard for a threat that no longer exists.

The Hippocampus

The **hippocampus** is another part of the brain that may play a role. The hippocampus is important for learning and remembering things.

When a child's abusive parent(s) overstimulate these important parts of the brain, the hippocampus and amygdala shrink; because these regions are smaller than average, the child will not be able to handle their emotions, especially feelings of shame and guilt, when they are adults.

Therefore, as the child of a narcissistic parent, you may struggle with reactivity and struggle to process things. You react to all the symptoms of post-traumatic stress disorder, and, therefore, depression, anxiety, bipolar, and even psychosis can also develop.

If you had a traumatic or unstable childhood, you might have disorders such as borderline personality, dependent personality, and avoidant personality disorder. Those are things that can develop as a result of a dangerous parent-child relationship.

Chapter 8:
What Is Trauma Bonding?

A trauma bond is a relationship between an abuser and their victim in which the abuser uses psychological and emotional manipulation to control their target and make them feel very dependent on them.

When there is physical or sexual abuse in a relationship, trauma bonding can happen at the same time. But even if you are being hurt, it may feel like you cannot just "walk away," even if the abuse is mental or a mix of the two.

Finding the tools necessary to break free of a trauma bond may take a long time for survivors. Due to fear for their safety or livelihood, they often stay longer than they should, resulting in even worse abuse before they can escape.

Who Is More Likely to Bond Over a Traumatic Event?

In a trauma bond, people who hurt people emotionally and in relationships usually get hurt, whether on purpose or not. Abusers often look for strong people, driven, smart, and able to think for themselves to feel better about themselves when they finally break themselves down.

Other things that could lead to trauma bonding are:

- People who are reliant on others,

- Whoever values "the good times" a lot and is quick to forgive,

- Anyone who was abused as a child or in a relationship. People whose attachments are messy, anxious, or avoidant,

- People tend to blame themselves even when there is strong evidence that they are not at fault,

- Problems with mental health, like depression, BPD, and anxiety, that already exist,

- People who worry about being alone,

- People who are easily hurt by being turned down.

Trauma bond survivors probably know intellectually that what is happening to them is wrong and that their relationship is painful and soul-crushing. Still, it is hard for them to see it as abuse.

Healing from abusive or traumatic relationships is not easy, but getting help from a professional can make all the difference. In the stages of trauma bonding that has been proposed, relationships often start out looking good but end up being abusive over time. This bond can greatly affect a victim's view of the world, how they see reality and their relationship with themselves.

These are the stages of bonding after trauma:

Love Bombing

Love bombing is a sudden, intense attempt to make a relationship feel like "we" by giving a lot of praise and compliments. This usually happens between the person who hurts someone and the person who gets hurt, but other people can also be involved. In some abusive situations, the abuser may not notice how they control the victim. However, this is usually not the case in a trauma bond.

Love bombing artfully sets the stage for abuse in a relationship with a history of trauma by:

- Letting the abuser play on the victim's feelings, hopes, dreams, and deepest desires. It is like saying, "Look at what I can give you, and no one has or will ever love you like this."

- Getting the victim to trust the abuser and let down their guard.

- Getting the possible offender and victim to feel good about themselves and validated.

- "Proving" that a person who hurts others means well.

- Creating a feeling of safety and stability.

Trust and Dependency

In this stage, the abuser may test the victim's trust and dependence on them on purpose. This usually makes the victim feel bad for asking questions about their partner. However, doubts are normal in any relationship; it takes time to know someone through what they say and do.

When you confront the abuser at this stage, you might get much flack for not appreciating everything they've done for you. This is why the love bombing stage is so important for creating dependence. The idea that the abuser is someone you can trust is a lie in a trauma bond.

Criticism

Trauma, according to research, confuses or shocks the brain, leading to a variety of biological as well as chemical changes and certain stress responses, including CPTSD, PTSD, other mental illnesses, substance abuse, changes in the brain parts like the limbic system, changes in hormones, changes in brain chemistry, and decreases in brain functioning. Some of these changes may occur on the inside and be more difficult to detect.

- "Wow, even when I mess up, he still loves and forgives me."

- "You are right, and I am so sorry for questioning you."

- "Because you want the best for me, you are right."

The trauma bond is held together by this back-and-forth dance of harsh criticism and over-apologizing.

Controlling and Misleading People

Gaslighting and manipulation are two common forms of psychological abuse that make victims question their reality and how they see it.

Gaslighters never take full or honest responsibility for their actions and tend to blame others. Gaslighters often seem calm, cool and collected immediately after pushing their target against the wall. Gaslighting is a behavior that abusers, like narcissists, sociopaths, and psychopaths, always engage in.

Fighting back or standing up to the abuser can feel like it will never lead to anything good, which can cause the target to act out abusively. This term refers to actions that look like abuse, but are done out of blind rage, the need to stay alive, or the need to protect one's mental health.

When their behavior turns physical, it is normal for victims of reactive abuse to feel guilty and worried. This makes the target of abuse question their identity even more because the gaslighting type of abuser wants to cut the victim off from anything or anyone, giving them a sense of security, normalcy, or independence.

Quitting

It is very normal for people who have been abused to start giving in at some point to avoid more fights. The "fawn" response to trauma, which includes bargaining and trying to make other people happy, may help keep the relationship somewhat stable.

Targets may have some idea that they are being manipulated, but that may not be enough for them to leave the relationship yet, because they may still wonder if they are to blame for the abuser's actions.

Depending on how long the relationship has been going on and what kind of psychological abuse is happening, the person being abused often becomes more emotionally and financially dependent on the person hurting them.

Many things, like safety concerns, make it hard for someone being abused to leave easily. It is normal to worry that an abuser's behavior will get worse when they feel like they are losing control, like when their victim threatens to leave or leaves. Many family fights can get worse and turn violent or deadly.

Losing Who I Am

During the stages of a trauma bond, there is a gradual loss of self, which causes pain and a break from the world we used to know. People who have just left an abusive relationship may not seem like themselves because they may have lost their sense of self and personal boundaries.

Trauma bonds can make you feel very alone because they can cause you to change in ways that are different from what your close friends and family are used to.

This mental damage could make you lose all confidence and even think about killing yourself. Many people have been going through this emotional torture, shame, and guilt for years, making it very hard to face and move on.

Getting Hooked On The Cycle

In trauma bonds, the stages can often repeat. For example, after a big fight, there may be a calmer time. However, at this moment of reconciliation, the abuser might apologize and start the love-bombing process again. This makes the target feel relieved and wanted, which makes them more dependent on this vicious cycle.

On the other hand, the abuser may shut down, avoid the victim, and stop showing love, affection, or attention to get the victim to apologize. When the blame is put on the abused person, they may do anything to get their abuser to like them again.

By doing this, the abuser gives the target the false impression that they are in charge. When the target wins back the abuser, they may think the abuser must love them, strengthening the idea that the sufferer is to blame.

What Happens to the Brain During These Stages?

Several biological changes and stress responses may result from trauma that confuses or shocks the brain. These include post-traumatic stress disorder (PTSD), other mental illnesses, substance abuse, and changes in parts of the brain, such as the limbic system, hormone changes, and brain chemistry. In addition, there might be changes occurring on the inside that are more difficult to observe.

Trauma can also have the following effects on the brain:

- Getting sick over and over,

- Outward signs of emotional pain, like panicking,

- Dissociation is an internal reaction,

- Fatigue,

- Brain fog,

- Sleep issues (i.e., nightmares, insomnia, etc.,)

- Fear of a repeat,

- Flashbacks,

- Avoidance.

How to Get Over a Bad Experience

When trying to escape a trauma bond or abusive situation, it is best to have easy accessibility to a support network or direct phone support from a reputed and reliable hotline to help deal with hard and confusing times.

Also, making a plan with your friends and family to leave quietly or without a fight while your narcissistic mother is away may help you .get out the door and stay as safe as possible since leaving a narcissistic relationship is the most dangerous time.

When to Talk to a Therapist

Therapy can be a great help, and there are practices like Trauma-Focused CBT designed to help people who have been abused. In addition, a therapist directory can be used to find a therapist.

Many survivors say that they thought about leaving their relationship or tried to leave it more than once before it finally ended. It is crucial to be honest about how hard it will be to leave the relationship and how strong the desire to go back can be.

Keep in mind that there are few studies on how much time or therapy will change how the relationship works. However, growth, recovery, and healing are all possible after a traumatic event.

In the end, I want to say that these stages of trauma bonding show that abusive relationships have a cycle of extreme highs and lows, which can make the victim feel alone, like they do not have an identity, and keep them in the relationship for too long. But it is possible to break a trauma bond, and help is easy to find.

Chapter 9:
How Can I Let Go of My Trauma and My Mother?

I t may be one of the most challenging actions you have ever considered, but in the end, it may become one of the most powerful, healthy, and affirming things you have ever done for yourself.

This is because allowing yourself to heal from the wounds inflicted by a narcissistic parent may be one of the most difficult actions you have ever contemplated taking. If you have exhausted all other conceivable courses of action and solutions to a problem, you may discover that the only option is to let go of whatever is bothering you. This can be a very uncomfortable situation to find yourself in.

You may have attempted various approaches to coexist with a narcissistic parent; nevertheless, if your connection with your mother has turned out to be too toxic and hampers your potential to be a happy, healthy, and independent adult, she is no longer a viable method. The force that has dominion over you—you are the only one who can determine whether or not to break through it.

In this chapter, I will provide you with seven strategies that will enable you to separate yourself from your narcissistic mother and go forward with self-assurance. These strategies will allow you to divorce yourself from your mother and move on with your life.

Put Your Requirements Before Those of Others

It is expected of the child of a narcissistic mother to put the narcissist's goals and desires ahead of their own, which will be obvious to anyone familiar with the pathological actions of a narcissistic mother.

This conduct must immediately stop. It will take a substantial amount of bravery and commitment to achieve this goal, but you owe it to yourself to put your requirements first for a change.

This does not imply that you should permit yourself to participate in self-indulgent or narcissistic behaviors. You are under no responsibility to respond to the humiliating criticisms that your mother has leveled at you or to answer the ridiculous requests that she has made.

Additionally, you do not reply to the requests that she has made. If her mental illness is detrimental to her psychological and physical well-being, making accommodations for it is less important. Make use of the following number as a guide to assist you in organizing your thoughts and emotions:

The ability of a narcissistic mother to manipulate her child's feelings, gaslight her child's perception of reality, and control her child's fundamental identity is the source of the narcissistic mother's power. Narcissistic mothers tend to have an unhealthy obsession with their feelings and those of their children.

You can make your path once you have distanced yourself from your narcissistic mother. You'll be able to recognize that her authority is illusory and that her control is open to question if you make some progress in removing yourself from the weight of her emotional baggage.

Cultivate a Singular Sense of Who You Are at Your Core

Narcissists view the world through the lens of their dominant personality and place themselves at the center of all that exists. This is remarkably accurate when it comes to their children.

When you finally come to terms with the fact that you are your personal and not an invention of hers, you will feel a sense of liberty and relief.

Establish Impregnable Limits That Cannot Be Crossed in Any Way

When they continuously violate the boundaries you have established, narcissists do not experience any regret or remorse. In addition, it may be challenging for the offspring of narcissists to develop and maintain healthy limits as they get older because they were not taught about healthy limits when they were growing up.

This makes it more likely that they will struggle to set clear boundaries. As a result, you ought to beef up your borders and keep your position firmly in place.

These non-negotiable constraints can be relatively easy, for example, by setting a cap on the number of characters or words that can be included in an email or text message.

Alternatively, these boundaries can be fairly strict, such as not being allowed to start a fight.

A break in contact that continues for an infinite amount of time. You will likely have to establish more strict boundaries if she cannot respect even the most fundamental ones.

Not Engaging in Revenge When There Is No Evidence of Wrongdoing

She will not give up her child without a fight since one of the things that the narcissistic mother fears the most is losing control over her child. Therefore, she will not give up her child easily. As a consequence of this, you should get ready for some resistance connected to the judgments you make.

Nevertheless, you must never forget that you were not the one who got yourself into this mess. Because of her behaviors, we have reached a breaking point, and if you begin to create boundaries and keep your distance from her, she will become angry and even threatening. It would be helpful if you would not give in to the need to feel guilty or sorry for yourself in response to her rage or self-pity.

When she finally realizes that her boundaries are unyielding, then and only then will she respect them. Over time, there is a chance that she will recognize their regard for one another.

Finally, try to refrain from blaming yourself for the problems in your relationship with your narcissistic partner. Now we are going to discuss topic number five. You are in no way responsible for the behavior of your mother.

Blaming yourself makes you feel guilty, making it more likely that you will let your guard down and cross your boundaries; instead, you should take responsibility for your actions and place the blame where it properly belongs.

Recognize This Sense of Self-blame Permeates Other Aspects of Your Life

Children raised by parents with narcissistic personality disorder are more prone to internalize the blame for anything that goes wrong in their relationships or the relationships of others.

Be very careful that you do not fall for this trick. The repeated actions that will inevitably result in failure Position six on the list: Encourage positive channels of expression.

Find methods that will enable you to express some of your emotions in a way that is therapeutic and good for you, and use those methods. For example, you may start a notebook by recounting your vacation with your mother, but you should not erase the anguish and rage you felt during that time.

Instead, put your creative skills to use by expressing those emotions in inventive ways that use the abilities you already have.

Decide on a New Routine/Way of Life To Pay Greater Attention to Your Physical Health

The practice of turning to these routines for solace when you are feeling anxious or depressed can be beneficial to both your mental and spiritual well-being. You could, for instance, give aromatherapy or massage a shot, start a yoga or meditation practice, improve the quality of your diet, or spend more time with individuals who positively influence your life.

Channel Your Emotions

It is impossible to stress the significance of identifying healthy outlets through which you can relax your mind and body through self-care and channel your feelings positively. While you are working through the mental and emotional challenges connected with letting go of your narcissistic mother, it is conceivable that it will not be enough to get you through this time.

You may find that you require additional help, particularly in the first phases of the process of detachment. You can seek professional counseling, look for support groups online, or do both if you feel it would be beneficial.

When you talk about your choices and your journey with others who have gone through something comparable to what you have been through, you may find that it helps you heal. Deciding to cut ties with your narcissistic mother will probably be one of the most difficult choices you will ever have to make.

However, on the other hand, it is undoubtedly one of the most liberating and wholesome choices you can make for yourself. You can begin mending yourself and creating space between yourself and your mother by using one of the many available ways.

This will help you get through the agony that you are currently experiencing. Believe in yourself and realize that you can make decisions that are personally beneficial to your growth.

Chapter 10:
How To Set Boundaries?

I think that setting boundaries is something that many of us struggle with. It must be considered that there is a difference between loving oneself and narcissism. Whenever you are about to love yourself and set boundaries, there is a chance you could feel like you are acting like your narcissistic mother; however, if you continue to set no boundaries, you will have no time to think about yourself.

You might be finding it hard to differentiate between doing what you need to do for yourself and being a narcissist who does not care about how your behavior affects others. It's maddening and horrible to accept that your reality is that you have a narcissist parent; instead of accepting how that possibly affects you, she is clamoring for you to understand.

Therefore, it's important for you to understand what constitutes "healthy selfishness."

"Healthy Selfishness"

There is a huge difference between someone who is narcissistically selfish to that extreme and someone who's learning to self-love and is learning to say, "This is what I want, this is what I think, and this is what I need."

If you are struggling to figure out where is the line between "healthy selfishness," which is self-love and self-care, and narcissistic self-love, the line for me is the idea that "I can love myself, but not to the exclusion of other people; I can include people in my life."

When you truly love yourself, you learn to honor yourself, and you can set boundaries. As you heal and are on the recovery path, you grow accustomed to holding people accountable for how they treat you. For example, you can be self-loving and have no contact with your narcissistic mother. That is an example of self-love and protecting yourself from her. That is not a malignant type of selfishness. That is healthy selfishness; that is self-care.

So, if you are on the path to understanding that you are responsible for making yourself happy, whereas a narcissist thinks you are supposed to make them happy, you are responsible for how they feel. If you are learning to honor yourself, love yourself, and make yourself happy, then you are on the right track and path.

Unfortunately, this is not very clear. Because when we start playing with boundaries and self-love, many of us have selfish, narcissistic parents who wonder, "Oh my God, am I turning into my mother?" Therefore, as you learn to love yourself, make sure you are taking responsibility for how you feel, and if you need to do something to take care of yourself, go out and do it.

When To Consider Other People When Exercising "Healthy Selfishness"

It is equally important to consider how your actions affect other people too. The line that you should draw is by asking yourself, "Are they considerate of me?"

Do not hold someone at the top of a list in your book in terms of priorities and how far you will go out of your way for them if you know that this person does not consider you to be important.

Become clear about whom you want in your life and whom you do not want, and understand what you need. Make sure you are responsible, and if you want something, find a way to get it for yourself or take care of yourself. If you want to feel appreciated, appreciate yourself. Only if you take care of yourself are you honoring yourself. If you are taking responsibility for your happiness, you are on the right track.

Dependence On Others

Dependence on others is fostered by a multitude of experiences: our narcissistic parents, the habit of constantly going above and beyond what is needed of us, and feelings of rejection when others fail to acknowledge our efforts; these all create a dependence on others to the point of being unhealthy. A co-dependent child will do anything to maintain a connection with another person and prevent the devastating emotional experience of being abandoned. They will develop an unhealthy obsession with obtaining praise and admiration. Codependency is built on the idea, "You should care more about what I think about you."

If you are in recovery, in a coaching program, or in therapy, you begin to understand this idea of boundaries and that boundaries are very healthy between children and parents, especially adults and their narcissistic parents.

What Happens When You Begin Confronting Your Narcissistic Mom?

Let's say you now realize your mum is being intrusive; there are things you do not want to tell her. Telling her things like, "I don't want to talk about it," will put her in a rage. But why is she angry? What is Mom doing? Pay attention to the technique because your mom is trying to get you to worry more about what she thinks about you than what you feel about her.

As long as you don't fall into that trap, you are good as long as you observe Mom. You could play with **detachment**, which is one of the keys to recovery.

Have a conversation with your Mom as an adult; get out of the amygdala, where your patterning is, and get to the frontal lobe, where your critical thinking lies.

The Confrontation

Remember, before initiating a confrontation, you are an adult; therefore, the most appropriate way to behave is as an adult: mature, composed and calm.

Here is an example of a hypothetical confrontation:

"Hello, mama. What's up? How are you? Yeah, well, I know you want to talk about it. Well, I do not owe you an explanation. I love you and all, but Mom, I am not seven anymore. I do not have to tell you why; I do not want to talk to you about stuff. It is enough to say I do not want to talk about it. So now you are using guilt against me. Mom, that is not cool. That is not going to help. You know what? You are upset right now. I can see that you are not having an easy time with me setting boundaries. But you know what, call me when you feel better or cool off, and I'll call you in a couple of days."

That is an example of the right things to say during a confrontation. I am not saying it is easy because setting boundaries with narcissistic moms is not easy, but nothing changes if you do not do it. Remember, nothing changes.

Nothing changes with one conversation. So, before conversing with Mom, remind yourself, "I am not six. And she is not the boss over me." Maintain good boundaries. You are not going into an adult's argument as a child anymore.

If your mom is overstepping her boundaries and is intrusive, sometimes what moms do is they'll send you things, or they'll send you cards rather than send your gifts in the mail. They might say,

95

"Come on, I want to take you shopping." Do not fall for it. What she is doing is trapping you. If you accept that gift, you owe her, and she will never forget that. Therefore, it is best to say things like, "No, Mom, I got it. Thanks very much. I appreciate it, but I cannot accept it, so I am returning it."

Establishing Limits

Limits can be established in four ways:

1. Define your limits. Before communicating or enforcing the boundary, ensure you know exactly what you need.

2. Set clear, reasonable, and consistent limits and expectations.

3. Just give them the facts; do not get into a blame game or a defensive stance.

4. Do some soul-searching and figure out what to do if your boundaries are not respected.

We know a relationship with a narcissistic mother is unhealthy but if you are still hesitant to end it or implement a no-contact policy. Then you can do the following:

1. Recognize that you have options (such as separating yourself emotionally and physically, reducing contact, avoiding being alone with the person, and engaging in self-care);

2.   Treat yourself with respect;

3.   Follow your gut.

There is, alas, no simple solution. However, it is important to recognize that setting boundaries is not about being mean or difficult and that sometimes you cannot keep certain people in your life if they are offended or angry by your decisions.

Boundaries help you avoid potentially harmful situations while retaining your independence and dignity. You deserve to treat yourself to these valuable items.

Chapter 11:
Cutting Your Ties

I f you choose to cut ties or have no contact with your narcissistic mother, read this chapter to understand the concept of no contact.

I think back to the early 2000s, the 90s the 80s; what we thought was normal back then is now being labeled as emotional, psychological, and narcissistic abuse. But why? I think it is because we eventually started to understand mental health. People started self-reflecting and wondering where did these thoughts/feelings come from and what stemmed from these dysfunctional family dynamics?

As a society, we started realizing what had happened to us as children, and we were ready to do something about it. It is unnatural not to be able to trust a mother, but it is not natural to fear a mother as something happens over an extended time or because you see how she reacts to certain situations. This can provoke fear inside of us. So, if we decide at some point that we want to initiate no contact, **here are three things to keep in mind.**

1. You Have To Let Go of Their Narrative

You have to let go of the narrative that they are creating about you while triangulating you and your siblings or by the narrative that they have created about you to their flying monkeys.

Many times, narcissistic parents will create stories about you to your other siblings or describe things they think you have done to them. Maybe you started noticing that your siblings do not talk to you anymore or the relationship is not healthy; we call this **triangulation**.

The narcissist is creating a wedge so that they are the point of contact for you and your siblings, but you and your siblings do not talk to each other because of the narrative they are creating about you.

Similarly, there is always going to be a false narrative that is going to be made about them with their friends or other relatives; therefore, you have to let go of caring about that narrative.

There were narratives placed on your life as a child, and that is why you have these inner critical thoughts of "I am not good enough, I am never going to get a good job." As a result, there's a reason why you have these inner critical thoughts that come from a narrative they placed on your life.

If you strip that narrative off so that you can find your authentic self, so you do not care about the description or story they are creating about you in their life, you will be focused on being the best person you believe you can be every day.

2. Stop Caring About Their Victim Mentality

At the root, anyone who is a narcissist will have a victim mentality. This is a tactic that they use to manipulate people and gain a narcissistic supply. A narcissist will always have that deep-rooted victim mentality.

Therefore, you need to let go and understand that that victim mentality is the root of narcissistic abuse and that you are going to take your focus back off the narcissists and bring back on the healing journey that you're on in your life.

3. It Is All About Our Perspective

It will be easy to take your focus off of yourself and concentrate it back on the narcissistic parent because that is what you're used to. Many people are very empathetic and trying to heal from narcissistic abuse, and a lot of us are people pleasers who care about what other people think or how they feel.

Therefore, you need to continue to cultivate the perspective that you are choosing yourself, not because you're selfish, but because you can change generational curses. I am taking what everyone else did, how they treated other people, and how they fell in line, and am wiping all that clean, healing yourself as a person, and having a clean slate.

If you have children or want to be the light in other people's lives, help other people through the abuse, but remember, it's all about your perspective.

The subconscious mind will always be attracted to whatever is negative and whatever is going to bring you down. You need your perspective to be, "I am choosing myself and a better life for myself," because that is how you can heal your mental health.

Understanding How You Feel About Your Narcissistic Mother

You care deeply feel for her because of your familial ties. Perhaps you feel obligated to remain in contact with her, or maybe you fear the impact of a no-contact policy on your family. What would happen to special occasions like holidays if you did this?

It is normal to have questions regarding all of this. It is not always easy to cut off all ties with relatives, especially your mother.

The following are some questions you could ask yourself:

- With this person, how do I feel deep down inside?

- May I cut down on my contact with her?

- In what ways do you think I can strengthen my limits?

- If I worked on my boundaries, would that improve things?

- Do I have the power to keep going despite the possibility that they will never change, or will this cause me too much pain?

The wisest course of action may be minimal contact rather than none. For example, you could test the waters with a trial period of reduced contact with your narcissistic mom to see how you respond.

How To Reduce Contact

You can begin by only spending time with this person while others are present, lending them money once they've paid you back, etc. Going silent could be the next best thing if you feel you have exhausted all other options.

When maintaining touch with this individual is causing damage to multiple parts of your life, cutting off all communication is the best course of action. It could refer to your physiological, psychological, financial, spiritual, or social well-being.

A safety plan and going emotionally cold with no contact at all are the recommended courses of action to take if your physical safety is in danger.

You can limit your interactions with a narcissistic parent or relative in several ways. Planning with a mental health expert can help you develop effective, risk-free strategies.

The **grey rock strategy** can help you set up if you want to take your time before completely cutting off communication.

The Grey Rock Strategy

In this mode of interaction, you are only sharing necessary information and doing it in a way that is about as engaging as a lump of grey rock. This also implies that you avoid lengthy discussions or arguments.

Finding places where you can "close the gate" may prove useful. For example, you could consider using your transportation to the lunch date rather than riding with her.

You could do so if you and your family felt more comfortable having get-togethers at a public venue than at home. You may cause each other much hurt by just stopping talking. There is a chance they share your feelings of loss and despair.

They may be unable to find the words to convey their sorrow adequately, but that does not mean it is not there. Say to yourself, "My relationship has been detrimental to my life for a long time. So that I may get well, I can no longer interact with her at this time."

Let a Loved One Know Your Decision

Boundaries and restricted interactions may not always be sufficient, however. Therefore, let other loved ones know your decision, which may necessitate changing your phone number or email address and unfriending them on social media.

Maintaining at least a glimmer of optimism that a relationship can improve is natural. You may benefit from lowering your expectations.

You have probably been through quite a lot by now. Know that it is possible to recover from whatever you are going through. As with any mental illness, a narcissistic personality disorder is multifaceted. Finding a support group and expanding your knowledge of narcissism may be helpful in your recovery.

A fresh outsider's viewpoint can often provide useful insight into a situation. Counseling can help in these situations. In doing so, you may get insight into the more subtle ways the relationship has affected you, which can pave the way toward healing the emotional wounds that resulted.

In addition, your therapist can help you examine how you may have contributed to the unhealthy patterns in your relationships. Attending therapy is a terrific method to gain insight, mend wounds, and develop personally.

Loss is loss, even if it occurs at the hands of the one inflicting the pain. To the best of your ability, be kind to yourself and give yourself time and space to deal with your loss. Keeping a journal, reducing your workload, or talking to friends and family may help.

Chapter 12:
How To Start Your Journey Toward Healing?

Y ou are probably wondering to yourself, what do you need to do to self-soothe? What are the issues that you need to remind yourself of? Firstly, it is important to remember that everyone's different, and everybody heals at a different tempo.

It might take one person a short amount of time to come to terms with what they experienced, while it might take another several months. That's completely understandable and it is not a symptom of weakness. The healing process is different for everybody.

The next thing to understand is that much of your negative thinking comes from the relationships you had with your parents because they did not treat you as they were supposed to.

For example, they did not teach you how to stay connected to yourself; therefore, you could not learn how to do that yourself. So when that negative thought comes, it is part of that wound that was repeatedly triggered as you were growing up.

The best thing to do, therefore, when you experience a negative thought, understand that it is not representative of you, "I will not give importance to this thought because it is not who I am. It is coming from my wounded self." This will allow you to disassociate from these thoughts and not hold onto them because when we do, that is where suffering happens.

Learning how to monitor where your ideas arise and how not to attach importance to every single one will allow you to live a peaceful, happy life.

The last thing that will allow you to heal is to learn how to endure your parents. This does not mean standing up to them and telling them what you think and how you feel and becoming angry.

Instead, it means expressing to someone what it is you need out of this relationship. If that someone cannot respect boundaries, then you need to alter that. It would help if you also changed your expectations of who that person is and what they are capable of.

Do Not Live in the Past

Your narcissistic mother might not have given you what she needed, but you cannot constantly live in the past. There is a wound that is in you. She possibly created that, but to heal, you must know where the wound is, what it looks like, and what you need to do to heal it.

Like any wound, you must clean it, put a Band-Aid on it, then take it off after a couple of days.

The first step to letting go of the past starts with accepting your mum for whom she is. That was your past, and working on creating a better future for yourself is your aim.

The only means to do that is by learning how to have a sincere relationship with yourself, giving yourself the things that you wish she would have and should have given you that would have allowed you to grow up and not be codependent. Now, it is up to you to heal those dark spots of yourself by yourself.

Chapter 13:
What Is the Best Therapy for Narcissistic Abuse?

S o far, I have talked in detail about how to accept our mothers, how to accept their narcissism and why they are the way they are, and the importance of focusing on yourself. I have also talked about accepting that we cannot change our narcissistic mothers and that we are not the cause of their behavior.

So, the question I will answer in this chapter is, what kind of therapy is best for someone who grew up with a narcissistic mother?

The Best Therapy for Someone Who Grew up With a Narcissistic Mother

There is no one therapy for narcissistic abuse because every person has a different set of circumstances and needs different therapy. So let's start with what you need, what therapy can do, and what you should try to find in therapy. It would help if you had a therapist who gets it when trying to find a way to cure your soul and heal from narcissistic abuse.

Many therapists do not do this as of now. A big reason is that nothing even close to this is taught in graduate school or clinical training. It is a pretty new area. Surprisingly, these problems have been around for a long time; however, this new way of systematically dealing with them by focusing on narcissistic abuse is new. There is still a tendency to be critical of someone who comes to therapy and says a narcissist has abused them. More than a few therapists will say things like, "Well, you should not diagnose your mother as narcissistic," or "Well, we cannot say they are narcissistic because they are not here to talk about it.

Let's talk about what you did to cause all of these problems." If we do not, the therapist might say, "Well, relationships are hard, so I'd love to hear your thoughts on that."

Did you ever see a therapist you thought did not fully understand narcissism or abuse? What parts of invalidation did you like? You might have talked about it in therapy, but it is very important.

Number One: Seek a Therapist Who Understands Narcissism

You need a therapist who understands the dynamics of narcissism and narcissistic relationships and does not take part in them. Dismissing you when you talk about dynamics such as gas lighting, love bombing, trauma bonding, etc., will be detrimental to your healing process. You should not have to be your therapist's teacher while your therapist is out.

There are many therapists who do not position themselves as experts in narcissism or narcissistic abuse. Therefore, take into consideration therapists who have experience with trauma or trauma-informed practices.

These therapists know that these patterns can leave you feeling confused and unsure of yourself. They will give you the time and space to make sense of these toxic relationship dynamics, grieve them, and work out what you want and how to deal with them.

Number Two: Seek a Therapist Who Makes a Space for the Unique Aspects of Narcissistic Abuse

Cognitive behavioral therapy focuses a lot on teaching a person how to change how they think to change how they behave. This might work, and it might work well. When a person's actions have nothing to do with his or her beliefs, we do not need a framework. But when we are talking about narcissistic abuse, we do need a framework.

Narcissism is hard to change, which is why gaslighting is a very real thing. This is because the person a narcissist abuses might be blamed for how they think.

Therefore, if you go to therapy and the therapist who is doing cognitive behavioral therapy, they will want to focus on changing how you think instead of teaching you that no matter how you y think, you are still being abused by a narcissist.

Narcissistic abuse needs to be explained and put into context in any therapy before only focusing on ideas like "you need to change your approach and way of thinking, and then you can change how you think forever." That will not stop someone from giving you a false story.

Number Three: Avoid Therapy Situations Where Keeping the Relationship Together Is a Big Part of the Plan

It is dangerous to try to make an abusive relationship work as it does not consider how toxic and constant narcissistic relationships are. It may also lead to feelings of guilt, failure, and self-blame.

Number Four: If You Cannot Find a Therapist Who Knows Much About Narcissistic Abuse, Look For One Who Specializes in Trauma

Therapists who are well-informed know how to work with people who have been through a traumatic or confusing experience. They do this from a place of validation, safety, and support, knowing how trauma affects the nervous system.

This point of view can be very helpful because part of being treated for abuse and trauma is making sure that the patient does not blame themselves for what happened.

Number Five: Work With Someone Who Knows More About Grief and Healing From Narcissistic Abuse Than You Do

Abuse is a deep dive into grief; it is not how we usually think of grief, such as for the dead; rather, grief over abuse can manifest itself as missed and lost experiences, grief over lost hope, and grief over lost time.

Number Six: Learn That There Are Ways To Help People Whom Narcissists Have Abused

They are what makes it. I will use a word for it, "**transtheoretical**." This is a framework that helps clients who are working with nurses.

A therapist can use abuse no matter what their theory is. You might find a psychodynamic, humanistic, cognitive behavioral, or eclectic therapist.

The therapist should understand the natural history of narcissistic relationships, the fact that narcissistic personalities are rigid and do not change, and other things like cognitive dissonance and trauma bonding.

The things that happen to someone who has been in a relationship with a narcissist, and to see it in that light. So, can this work be done by any therapist? If they are willing to see it for what it is.

Number Seven: Find a Therapist Who Will Work From a Culturally Aware Point of View

To understand narcissistic abuse, the therapist needs to be able to work from a culturally aware point of view. Because of what it does to a person, the patient needs a therapist who understands the complexities of race, ethnicity, social class, and gender. If someone is already being gaslighted by society, it makes the gaslighting in their relationship feel even worse.

Number Eight: Stay Away From/Reconsider a Therapist Who Makes Your Therapy About Them

I agree that having been abused by a narcissist gives a therapist a more informed and empathetic view of the situation. However, every survivor's story is different. For example, things that worked for me and parts of my story might not work out for you. Therapy is your space, story, and experience, so give it to yourself.

If a therapist doubts your experience based on theirs or gives you advice based on theirs, remember, your therapy is not meant to be a place for therapists who are also narcissistic abuse survivors to talk about how brave they are. You might well want to hear the story, but after that, it is your time.

Number Nine: Even an Expert in Narcissistic Abuse Recovery Might Not Always Be a Good Fit for You

They might be a good therapist for someone else, but if it does not feel good for you, they are not a good fit for your needs. They might call themselves an expert, but finding the right therapist is now always about credentials. It can also be about finding the right professional whom you can connect with on this psychological level and maintain a good professional relationship with.

If the therapy does not make you feel good, stop going. You have the right to leave and look for someone else. Do not be afraid of upsetting the therapist.

Number Ten: Consider Adding Support Groups to Therapy

Some support groups might not have good people running them. So, if the group does not feel right or safe, you should not feel like you have to stay with it. Peer spaces and supportive spaces can help you heal and grow and also help you get something out of them. Rank and a sense of belonging came from knowing that other people had been through the same thing.

Number Eleven: You Have To Do Work Between Sessions

I am one of many people who think journaling is a great idea, whether it's documenting rituals and routines for making lists and cleaning, toxic people, reading to learn about mindfulness, etc. This is about how your whole life can change.

Even though therapy is important, what a person does in the 167 hours between sessions is even more important.

Number Twelve: Be Wary of Services That Promise To Fix Narcissistic Abuse in Six Weeks, etc

Healing is unique to each individual. It is always a process. Some people need months, and others need years. And that is all right.

Work with a therapist who can help you figure out if you are having other problems, like anxiety, depression, or a substance use disorder, and then helps you deal with those problems along with the narcissistic abuse patterns you are going through.

Abuse and the other things you are going through are linked, and both need to be fixed. It is not as simple as saying, "Once we take care of your anxiety, we'll come back and talk about that." Narcissist abuse is a problem that must be dealt with immediately.

Concerning therapy for narcissistic abuse, a good model includes practices that take trauma into account. Trust that the therapist will not blame or tell you that you are wrong.

Grief work is a part of good therapy. People should be taught about the patterns of narcissism and how they are important as it relates to you. Awareness about things like gas lighting, how to fortify and strengthen yourself, and how to deal with rumination.

Awareness about intersectional and cultural issues important to your gender, race, and gender. You name it, awareness of psychosocial issues like domestic violence, problems with older people, custody problems, and a connection to useful resources. Your therapist does not have to know much about this to help you. That is all they need to know.

These are important things you should look for or talk to someone about to help you understand your emotions.

Chapter 14:
Is CBT Good For Me?

C ognitive behavioral therapy (CBT) can work well for survivors of narcissistic abuse and is often used to help people recover. With the help of a therapist, you can start to:

- Find out why you put up with abuse;

- Learn how to deal with stress, so you can handle abusive relationships;

- Don't give in to the urge to stay in touch with an abusive person;

- Be open and honest with the people in your life about the abuse you've been through;

- Determine if you're showing signs of anxiety, depression, or other mental health problems;

- Deal with and get past any thoughts you might be having about self-harm or suicide.

But for some people, CBT doesn't deal with the fact that trauma leaves a mark on the Amygdala, a part of the brain. For example, a person with severe social anxiety may have been traumatized when they were young. This trauma may have worsened as the person got older because the traumatized child did not have the skills to deal with society as an adult.

This person's fight, flight, freeze, and adrenaline response happens every time they meet another person (e.g., when they leave the house). This means that the sympathetic nervous system is "on" most of the time the person is awake. This kind of person needs to rest and be safe so that the parasympathetic nervous system can heal the body and brain. Because of this, they feel the need to be alone and often can't get anything done because getting through the day is so hard on them.

Others call these people "lazy," and CBT therapists might often tell them to "go for a daily walk," "get a job," "get a hobby," and "socialize," all of which puts the person in more situations that remind them of the trauma.

Eventually, this wears the person out, and they have a nervous breakdown in which they feel like they can't handle anything, cry every day, often think about killing themselves, and blame themselves for not "trying harder." So, it might stop you from getting the right diagnosis (Complex PTSD) because CBT might try covering up, hiding, and not believing your symptoms.

I'll say it again, **if the relationship with the therapist does not feel good, you should leave, not stay**. We are all the right fit for every client. It is hard for people whom a narcissist has abused to value themselves enough to tell a therapist that something does not feel right. But it does not always work out that way, and finding someone who works for you is important.

Most people come out of this situation wiser, stronger, and with a few battle scars. But do not forget what Rumi says about those wounds, "The light comes in through these wounds."

So, let therapy be a place for you to stand up for yourself, build your strength, and talk about what has hurt you. It should be a place to help you, not to blame or shame you. So, I hope you found the answer to your question about therapy.

Chapter 15:
Find Yourself

I f narcissists raised you, there is a chance that you do not know who you are and struggle with your identity. Mothers who are full of themselves treat their kids like extensions of themselves and do not want their kids to be their own people.

But because your mother's narcissism made you into the person she wanted you to be, you might feel that it is wrong to have your thoughts, feelings, and actions or to live the life you want. You might have trouble with negative self-talk, self-doubt, and other negative feelings that you might link to your sense of self-worth.

However, it is possible to find yourself again after enduring narcissistic abuse. Part of getting better from narcissistic abuse is trying to find and get to know yourself again. And just as how it took a long time to take away your sense of self, it will take time to build it back up. But it is possible with time, work, and hope.

In this chapter, I'll tell you what you can do to find yourself after a mother has hurt you narcissistically. This will not be easy, and it might take a lifetime, but it is important for getting better. As you keep improving and living, you will keep learning more about yourself. This will make you want to be your true self and live a happy life, even though you may still have questions about "who I am?"

Who You Are?

"Who are you?" seems like an easy question to answer. But the answer to that question could not be more complicated. How would you respond if someone asked, "Who are you?

If you have been abused by a parent who only cares about themselves, it is even harder to figure out who you are because you have only ever been the person your mothers wanted you to be.

When kids grow up with caring mothers, they can find and develop their interests, hobbies, passions, dreams, and goals. But the children of narcissistic mothers end up living in their mothers' shadows, doing what their mothers want them to do and becoming who their mothers want them to be.

Finding out who you are is not just a journey for people who grew up with narcissists. Everyone goes through this at some point in their lives. As we go through new things, we learn more about ourselves. So even though narcissists abuse you, you will continue to find yourself as long as you live.

How To Find Yourself After Being Mistreated by a Narcissist Mother

Use a journal to help you through this process of finding yourself after being abused by a narcissist

A journal will help you track what you learn about yourself as you go. It will also be a good tool even when you think you are done with the process. Think about how your experiences have changed who you think you are. Your sense of self is how you feel about the things that make you who you are, like your personality, skills, interests, beliefs, values, and passions. Abuse from a narcissist hurts your sense of self and makes you feel bad in other ways.

Write about the narcissistic abuse you went through and how it affected you. Mothers probably greatly impact how their kids turn out as adults. The difference is between encouraging someone and forcing them to do what you want. Knowing the difference by writing things down in a journal can help you figure out if your interests or passions came from a healthy influence or from someone trying to trick you.

Understand How the Abuse Made You Feel About Yourself

Narcissists get their sense of self from what others say and how much they like them. So their wants, needs, and values often depend on other people, especially those they were trying to control at the time. So, in a way, they do not know who they are.

Your sense of who you are is probably similar. It might take on the traits of other people, like your mothers, instead of your own. However, it is a little different because she is your mother, and you look up to her. Therefore, she can use that power to tell you not to do or to do certain things.

You might not have been allowed to play with some toys, wear particular clothes, watch certain shows, or do other things. Instead, your mother probably made you do things she thought would look good for her. Or, she made you do it because she wanted to feel what you were feeling.

Even as an adult, you might not have been allowed to choose a certain major, attend a certain school, work at a certain job, or date certain people. It had to be something your mother liked and met her expectations. You probably haven't been able to do or try many things you wanted to in your life. But she has you under her control and is getting you to do what she wants. She made you into the kind of person she wants you to be. So, much of who you are now was made by your mother. She is probably written all over your actions, thoughts, hobbies, interests, passions, and things you have done well.

Get Away From What the Abuse Did to You

Learning how your experiences have changed you helps you see how your past has made you who you are now. It helps you figure out what is you and what was caused by the abuse.

You might think that all the bad things you feel are who you are or a big part of who you are. But remember, *they do not define you.* They were made that way because of how they were raised. You only think that because that is what your narcissistic parent told you repeatedly. Again, it is not who you are.

Avoid the false, automatic ways you have learned to react to people and your environment. Instead, try to see that the negative self-talk, self-doubt, self-hatred, and lack of confidence are not you.

Understand that how you feel about yourself and others is probably not because of who you are but simply because of how you were raised. Therefore, *it does NOT define you.*

Under all the hurt and pain you have been through, there is a person. Do not let what you have done and been through define who you are. If you do that, you'll always be a victim.

However, you do not have to let it happen to you. You can get your life and yourself under control. After narcissistic abuse, you can find yourself.

Connect With How You Feel

It can be hard to find yourself when you have trouble recognizing, controlling, and dealing with your emotions because your emotions may control your actions or thoughts.

Emotions can greatly affect how we look at ourselves and our world. Nevertheless, to find yourself again after being abused by a narcissist, you need to get in touch with how you feel.

So, if you want to know how you feel, you need to understand how to deal with your feelings healthily. When you know how to deal with your feelings healthily, you can see your feelings, thoughts, and situations more objectively. Therefore, it's a very important step in finding yourself.

Get Support

You do not have to go through healing and finding yourself alone. You can get help from a clinical psychiatrist.

A professional can help you make sense of your past, understand your feelings, and find ways to heal.

Consider Your Values

Once you can tell the difference between what you learned from your mothers and what makes you who you are, think about your values and beliefs.

Your narcissistic mother probably taught you a lot of beliefs and values that you thought were right or took as your own. However, just because it was or still is the right way for them to live does not mean it is the right path for you.

Think about what your mothers stood for and what they believed in.

Now Consider Yours

Do your values and beliefs resemble those of your mothers? Is it what you believe in and value?

Again, it is normal for our mothers to affect us. And naturally, there is nothing wrong with that. But there needs to be room for independence.

Did you ever question your beliefs and values? Or did you agree because you thought it was true?

Usually, we have to have some experience that makes us feel that way before we can value and believe in something. It is valuable because of this.

I used to think that my "biological" family was the most valuable entity in the world. "Blood is thicker than water," I was always told. I still care about my family, but what I care about now is my chosen family, which may or may not share DNA.

What's important is the love and relationship we have with each other. As you adopt certain values, morals, or beliefs, keeping a healthy amount of curiosity and skepticism is important.

Think About Your Strengths

I want you to think about the things you do well. Think about what you are good at, what you have studied, and what you have accomplished. You are good enough, but you have to believe it. So give it some thought: what makes you good enough?

Attempt to think of at least ten things. They can be traits, skills, an accomplishment, or anything else.

This might seem like a dull and silly thing to do, or it could be one of the hardest things you might have to do. Nevertheless, it is just to let you know that you are fine. And even if you do not believe it, you know it is true deep down. You know that all the bad things you feel or think about yourself are lies that your narcissistic parent told you.

If you are having trouble, you can ask a friend or family member for help making a list.

Now, upon completing this list, pull it out whenever you doubt yourself or feel you are not good enough. Or, even better, try this exercise again. You need to make it a routine to think about the good things about yourself, even if it seems like a total waste of time.

Decide What Your Passions, Interests, and Hobbies Are

Your interests, passions, hobbies, and everything in between probably reflect your mother's or other people's interests, passions, and hobbies.

Think about all the things you liked to do as a child or wanted to try but could not because you were afraid or were not allowed to. Then, write them all down and find a time to do them.

If you cannot think of anything, it is time to look around and try new things. First, go out and find what you love and what you want. Then, go out and try something different.

Find something new to do. Try out a sport. Go to some new places. Help out different groups by giving your time. Do a variety of jobs. This can help you figure out how much you like or dislike something. Keep looking around. More will be found the more you try.

Are you more artistic or practical? Why not both? Do you like working with your hands? Do you like hobbies that get you up and moving, or do you prefer ones that make you think more?

You can live and have new experiences if you try new things and put yourself out there. This does not have to be anything crazy, by the way.

Consider What You Want From Life

Think about what you want from life. Or, if it helps, try picturing what you want the future to be like.

To be clear, this is NOT the same as guessing or imagining what you think the future will be like. Instead, think about what you want to happen in the future. Consider the following:

- What are your goals in life?

- What kind of life do you want?

- Describe how you want to feel.

- Where are you going?

- Whom would you like to hang out with?

- What are you trying to do?

Please list what you want, no matter how cliche it sounds. It could be to get a job, be with a certain person, go to a certain place, or reach a certain goal. Anything you want is valid.

If you cannot think of anything, write down what you can do to answer these questions. How do you find the answers to these questions? What do you have to do or go through first?

It might take a lifetime to figure all of this out. And that is all right. Even though you do not know what will happen, it is important to keep moving forward and be true to yourself.

Accept Yourself as You Are

Try not to judge who you are, no matter what you find out or do not find out about yourself.

You might find something that goes against what or who you thought you were. Or, you might find something about yourself that your mothers might not like, immediately making you feel guilty or ashamed. But that is the whole point. To figure out who YOU are, NOT what your mother thought you should be.

Be real and honest with yourself, even if it is something you did not think you were or that your mother might have made you against.

So what if you are not good at some things, or your mother did not like what you wanted from your life, or whom you wanted to date? As long as you are now happy and healthy, it should not matter what other people think.

And if you ever change your belief about how you feel about something, that is fine, too. Even if you like or dislike something today, you might feel differently about it tomorrow. Even if you liked or disliked something as a child, that does not mean you still feel the same way about it now.

We change and grow based on what we do and what we learn. Every day, we learn something that might change how we see ourselves and the world. So you cannot always be you. Every second of every day,

128

you are different. The point is to enjoy who you are and what makes you who you are right now.

Figure Out How To Love Yourself

Good mothers help their kids feel good about themselves and love themselves. Unfortunately, you did not get that chance, which is too bad. But that does not mean it is impossible to get.

I do not expect you to understand self-love immediately because it is hard.. But you can find different ways to love yourself and slowly build up how much.

When you love yourself, you'll start to see what's good about who you are. You'll start to do things that will help you get ahead. So, finding ways to love yourself will help you find yourself again after being abused by a narcissist and heal you.

You are on a journey to discover what you want from this life and what makes you happy. Just doing that is a way of loving yourself. So, trying to find yourself will lead you to love yourself, and the same goes for loving yourself. You might not quite love yourself yet. And that is all right. But try to be kind to yourself, at least. Practice self-care. Give yourself the same kindness, compassion, and attention you would give to your younger self. Self-love will come out in the end, whether you are aware of it.

Do Whatever You Want

I know it is hard and that people are harsh out there, but try to be at least okay with who you are when you are in your own space with people who matter. Because if they care about you, they'd love you for who you are.

It is easier said than done, but it does not matter what anyone else thinks. If someone says they love you, they will accept whatever decisions you make as long as they do not hurt anyone. It is important that you are healthy and happy.

You may finally be yourself and experience life to the fullest right now. So do things that please you. This could be:

- Getting close to people who love and care about you.

- Making your home a safe and pleasant place to be.

- Visiting and going wherever you want.

- Doing whatever you want.

- Doing what YOU want to do.

- Being Who You Are

Getting to know yourself is all about being yourself. It could take some time. So try to take things slowly. But, again, you did not become who you think you are overnight. You will need some time to get past the facade your narcissistic parent made for you.

Whether or not a narcissist mistreated you, you are not alone in your journey to find yourself. In addition, learning to know oneself takes a lifetime. We are always evolving, moving, and improving, whether conscious of it or not. It all depends on how eager you are to try and learn new things.

Try as hard as you can to escape from your parents/mother. And try not to let what you have done and what you have been through define who you are.

You are not your parent. You are not the bad treatment you got. And the abuse hasn't made you the symptoms, mental conditions, or bad things it has made you feel. So learn to be yourself, even if it is hard. Mothers who do their jobs right ensure their kids can be their people.

Try to develop your individuality. Finding yourself might take your whole life. But every little thing you learn gives your life more meaning and pleasure. And as you go on, do things that make you happy and stay true to yourself, no matter how many mysteries there are.

Chapter 16:

Other Complementary Treatments for Post-traumatic Stress Disorder (PTSD)

A lthough conventional therapy is useful, some patients find that complementary and alternative medicine, sometimes known as CAM, is highly effective in managing their post-traumatic stress disorder.

Common forms and methods of therapy

It is difficult to include all of the therapies that fall under the banner of complementary and alternative medicine (CAM), but some of the more frequent modalities include the following:

- chiropractic,

- acupuncture,

- massage,

- the practice of naturopathic medicine,

- yoga,

- tai chi,

- qigong,

- guidance with nutrition,

- supplementation,

- herbalism.

The conditions that CAM may assist support are as diverse as the modalities it uses.

These might be things like:

- sleep,

- pain,

- mood disorders,

- stress,

- anxiety,

- reducing or increasing one's weight,

- conditions that have been identified as being chronic or both.

Sometimes practicing yoga and meditation can help reduce stress to the point where a person no longer has to take any medicine.

However, complementary and alternative medicine (CAM) is not necessarily a substitute for conventional care. In other cases, such as when dealing with significant illnesses like PTSD, biological measures still need to be taken.

Alternative and complementary medicine (CAM) is gaining popularity, and evidence supports its presence in the healthcare industry. Many persons coping with PTSD have found that CAM is beneficial.

One study conducted in 2013 showed that 39% of 599 persons with PTSD reported adopting complementary CAM treatments, such as meditation and relaxation techniques, to assist ease symptoms.

Therapies are available for patients who have post-traumatic stress disorder.

Mediation is not generally regarded as one of the primary therapies for PTSD, even though it could be beneficial in conjunction with other types of therapy.

The most effective treatment for PTSD continues to be talk therapy, according to a study conducted in 2017 that investigated the effects of yoga and meditation. However, according to the opinions of several specialists, the following methods are especially useful:

Treatment That Focuses on Cognitive Processing (CPT)

CPT focuses on how trauma may have distorted your thinking, such as "It is all my fault" or "No one can be trusted." This approach can help you balance honoring your feelings and challenging extreme beliefs. CPT focuses on how trauma may have distorted your thinking.

Extended Contact Over Time (PE)

Through guided confrontations, physical education can help you lessen your emotional response to triggers. For instance, if you went to therapy after being in a vehicle accident, your therapist could have you view films of cars and perform relaxation techniques during the session.

Desensitization and Processing Through Eye Movements

EMDR, or The Eye Movement Desensitization and Reprocessing treatment, tries to alter how your brain stores painful memories to prevent these memories from resurfacing. For instance, an EMDR therapist can instruct you to do a series of eye movements while concentrating on a particular memory.

Both CPT and PE are specific kinds of cognitive behavioral therapy (CBT), which assists patients in addressing unhelpful patterns of thinking and behavior. However, although cognitive behavioral therapy (CBT) can still be helpful to persons with PTSD, the review described above indicated that it was less effective than its trauma-focused modifications.

Meditation is a technique that can assist you in concentrating your thoughts and gaining a more acute awareness of your:

- self,
- one's ideas and internal experiences,
- surroundings,

- Moment-to-moment needs.

What you decide to concentrate on during meditation may be influenced by the meditation you engage in, and the several styles of meditation may each provide its practitioners with a unique set of advantages.

Different forms of meditation, such as the following, have shown some promise in reducing the symptoms of post-traumatic stress disorder (PTSD):

Meditation Focuses on Being Mindful

The term "mindfulness" means a condition of mind in which a person can recognize their thoughts, feelings, and physiological sensations without passing judgment. Being an observer in your thoughts is how some individuals describe what this feels like.

The practice of mindfulness meditation uses this state to help you restrict your focus on what is occurring in the here and now. If you work on increasing your awareness of the now and now, you may find it easier to root yourself in the more secure here and now, even when disturbing memories surface.

In a nutshell, it is possible that taking your "mental eye" off the future will help your anxiety fade away.

Mantra Meditation

In the practice of mantra meditation, you will focus your attention by verbally repeating a sound, phrase, or mantra. You can select any positive affirmation phrase or sound that resonates with you.

Mantra meditation does not require you to adhere to any particular religion or spiritual practice; however, as you become more experienced with the practice, you will most likely become familiar with some spiritual terminology.

Mantra meditation has been shown to alleviate hyperarousal symptoms, such as anxiety and muscle tension. When you begin to relax your body, you may find that you can also relax your mind more easily, and vice versa.

Meditation Focused on Loving-Kindness

Meditation on metta, which means "loving-kindness," can help increase feelings of love and kindness toward oneself and others. During this time spent in meditation, you might visualize yourself getting well-wishes from your loved ones and sending them mental best wishes of happiness in return.

It will likely not surprise you that regularly surrounding yourself with positive energy can improve your mood and help you feel better.

According to a small pilot study conducted in 2013 on 42 veterans who have PTSD, loving-kindness meditation may enhance positive emotions, reduce the symptoms of depression, and foster self-compassion. These outcomes may help counterbalance the feelings of irritability, sadness, and self-criticism you might experience due to PTSD.

According to the review from 2017 that was mentioned up top by the study, meditation has the potential to have a moderate effect on the symptoms of PTSD by assisting with the following:

- A reduction in levels of stress

- Boost mood

- Attempt to lessen the number of distracting thoughts

The authors found that there was not a considerable difference between the various forms of meditation. However, they also observed that meditation does not appear to have as large of an effect as the first-line therapy approaches discussed earlier in this paragraph.

Despite this, it appears to have effects comparable to medication management, and It is the second-line treatment for PTSD. Or we can say it is highly unlikely that meditation will be effective in treating the symptoms of PTSD on its own, but it may be useful when combined with other treatments.

Are You Thinking About Giving Meditation a Shot but Unsure How To Start?

Try beginning with this simple form of meditation on breathing:

1.   Find a place to sit where you'll feel safe and comfortable if your stress level rises to an uncomfortable level at any point throughout the day. It could be a secluded nook in the room where you will not feel as exposed to people. It could even be a location where you are in the company of reliable people. Also, when you find a seat just right for you, whether a cushion or a chair, make sure that your back is supported while still comfortable.

2.   Begin by keeping your eyes open.

3.   Take a few long, slow breaths. Start by blowing your nose. And then out through your mouth. At this point in the practice, close your eyes as a standard first step.

Do not be afraid to give this exercise a shot today while keeping your eyes open. If doing so makes you feel more at ease, you can adapt the procedure to better suit your needs and make it your own.

Let's focus on our weight being supported by the ground or the chair and by the physical contact points around us. Take note of the chair pressing against your back.

Are those your legs or feet pressing against it? Your hands are resting in your lap. Take note of the tension. Temperature. Sensations.

Energy. Also, I'd appreciate it if you could focus elsewhere for a little while.

If Your Mind Wanders To Other Things

See if you can observe your thoughts, whether they are images, flashbacks, or feelings, rather than getting caught up in them, instead of making up a narrative about these pictures.

You probably have the expression, "Your thoughts are not the same as yours." The same is true about the fact that you are not your trauma. You are the observer of both your thoughts and your traumatic experiences. Having this knowledge can help you have a fighting chance by preventing you from getting caught up in the thoughts and emotions that come to the surface.

Therefore, by engaging in this practice, you can gradually improve your capacity to observe your thoughts, which, in turn, will enable you to exert greater control over the contents of your mind. Granting you, the real you, greater control over both the experience you have within yourself and the actions you take.

However, for the time being, let's divert our attention away from noticing these thoughts and bring it back to the present. Now we will discuss breath.

Breathing

Start paying attention to each breath. Take a breath in and let it out as each one goes by. Take note of the rising and falling feelings associated with the breath. In addition to that, there is nothing else that must be done here.

There is nothing you need to change about the way the breath sounds. Just pay attention to the passage of each breath. Let go of your attention here while maintaining an open awareness. Keep an eye on your breath and be aware.

If you notice a thought trying to sneak in, gently redirect your attention back to the breath. Let go of any attempts to concentrate or control your attention. Just give in and let the mind do what it wants to. Pay attention to your requirements whenever you meditate, especially if you have PTSD.

If you find sitting cross-legged uncomfortable, you can try lying down instead. However, you should keep your eyes open if the act of closing them makes you feel vulnerable.

Always keep in mind that the level of ease that you experience is more important than following any rules.

Patients find that by practicing mindfulness, dealing with traumatic experiences can become an integral part of their daily lives, and difficult emotions can become more manageable. Try a more condensed version of this mindfulness practice if the previous one is too challenging.

Additional treatment options for PTSD that are complementary in nature

Meditation is not the only complementary and alternative medicine (CAM) method that can help address the symptoms of PTSD. Additional methods that could be added to your treatment toolbox include the following:

Yoga

To induce a state of calmness, yoga relies on several techniques, including mindfulness, breathing, and stretching. In addition, yoga has been shown to help people with post-traumatic stress disorder (PTSD) manage their physical and emotional stress.

For instance, a study conducted in 2014 included sixty-four women with treatment-resistant PTSD. One-half of the participants attended women's health education classes, and the other half participated in trauma-informed yoga. After receiving treatment, the women in the yoga group reported experiencing improvements in the following areas:

- A capacity for withstanding the physiological manifestations of fear (such as muscle tension)

- Understanding of their current emotional state

- The ability to acknowledge and tolerate unpleasant feelings

The members of the control group also reported some of these improvements. However, during the second half of treatment, they reported returning their PTSD symptoms, whereas those in the yoga group reported a long-lasting improvement.

Biofeedback

During the biofeedback process, monitors will track your biological functions, such as your heart rate and body temperature, as you engage in relaxation exercises.

A therapist specializing in biofeedback will guide you through several relaxation exercises while the biofeedback device demonstrates how effective each one is in real time.

You might find it easier to learn these techniques and apply them effectively if you have this immediate feedback and positive reinforcement at your disposal.

Although there have only been a few studies done on biofeedback, the results have been encouraging. For example, in one study conducted in 2015, eight participants were given either trauma-focused CBT or CBT combined with biofeedback.

Even though both groups reported experiencing improvement, the group that participated in biofeedback experienced a significantly more rapid reduction in the symptoms of PTSD.

Acupuncture

Needles are inserted into certain points on the body in acupuncture, a form of traditional Chinese medicine. Altering your autonomic nervous system, responsible for regulating unconscious bodily functions like your heart rate and breathing, is said to be one-way acupuncture can help reduce stress.

There is still a lack of evidence supporting the benefits of acupuncture for PTSD. In many studies, there is no adequate representation of a control group.

A systematic review conducted in 2018 looked at seven acupuncture studies that did include control groups; however, the authors concluded that the majority of these studies still had a "very low" quality of evidence.

Of course, this does not inevitably imply that acupuncture is ineffective. On the contrary, many people find it useful, so giving it a shot is probably a good idea, especially considering the low risk of trying it.

EFT Emotional Freedom Technique

EFT stands for "Emotional Freedom Techniques," although most people call it "Emotional Freedom Technique." EFT is also called "tapping." Gary Craig, an engineer who went to Stanford and studied acupressure healing techniques (even though he wasn't a therapist), devised EFT.

Craig created a simple method that involved "tapping" on some essential acupuncture and acupressure points while thinking about a problem.

The acupressure points used in EFT come from Traditional Chinese Medicine (TCM), a way of healing developed through observation and trial and error over thousands of years. You don't have to understand

TCM or believe in a particular spiritual philosophy or religion to use EFT.

Gary Craig has since gone beyond his original EFT formula and the tapping to work on a more spiritual level with what he calls the "Unseen Therapist" that he thinks everyone has inside them. But you can still find his original EFT formula on his website and learn it for free.

Benefits of EFT

EFT benefits many issues, including anxiety, depression, phobias, and even physical illnesses. EFT can also help people with PTSD.

Traditional Chinese Medicine (TCM) says that blocked energy in the "meridian" channels is often the cause of negative emotions. In EFT, tapping makes new energy flow (called "chi") and removes emotional blockages. EFT might help bring down Cortisol levels.

Once the energy, or chi, starts to flow, it can help lower cortisol, a stress hormone that can cause problems when it's made in large amounts. Cortisol also makes stomach fat, so reducing it can help you lose weight. EFT may help reduce the symptoms of PTSD. EFT works exceptionally well for treating panic attacks, bad dreams, and phobias.

If you have severe PTSD, you should seek help from a qualified EFT practitioner or licensed therapist with experience with EFT. EFT may help with pain caused by narcissistic abuse that shows up in the body. From what people have told me, EFT seems to help a lot with pain relief. EFT may help heal suffering from childhood.

Note, you should expect that you will need more than one EFT session to heal from narcissistic abuse. EFT can fix some issues almost instantly, but for more complicated problems, you might need to work on more than one layer (in traditional EFT, these are called "aspects.")

If tapping on one part of the body doesn't help, try tapping on another. For example, let's say you were in a car accident and tapped on your fear. This only helped a little. By focusing on something more specific, like "feeling trapped in the car," you've gotten to the root of the problem. EFT is a great, free tool that anyone can use to help heal their emotions after being abused by a narcissist.

Getting Professional Support

Contacting a mental health professional is a good next step to take if you notice that the symptoms of PTSD are beginning to interfere with your day-to-day life.

You can search in the following places for a therapist or counselor:

- It would be best if you inquired with your healthcare team for a referral.

- Check the website of your insurance provider to see if they have any trauma therapists in their network

- Stop by your neighborhood's community mental health clinics to learn about the various support options available.

- Give some thought to the various online therapy platforms

If you find that you are struggling to cope with the symptoms of PTSD, incorporating a meditation practice into your treatment plan may be beneficial.

Remember, meditation cannot usually take the place of traditional talk therapy as the primary form of treatment. Working with a therapist who specializes in the treatment of PTSD is, in most cases, the best way to make improvements that are likely to be long-lasting.

Chapter 17:
Are You An Angry Victim of Narcissistic Abuse?

When you are a victim of narcissistic abuse, your anger can increase and decrease, rising and down like a roller coaster. Sometimes it can be so bad that you cannot sleep or eat, and other times it just simmers below the surface, causing resentment, which feeds the anger.

Unfortunately, it is a cycle when you are in a narcissistic relationship, especially with your mother.

Many people who have experienced and survived narcissistic abuse end up can like the person who commented the abuse: full of anger and other feelings that steal their happiness.

It is bad enough to be in a place where you are being abused and feeling all these bad things, but it is not right, especially if you can get away from that place but are still suffering.

Therefore, you need to know what anger is and how to control it.

What Is Anger?

Anger is a normal part of emotional healing; we must go through it to get out of it. If you look at people who have been abused at home, they do not leave until they are forced to.

When you find the strength to leave, your anger pushes you away. You are finally done, and you are leaving. That is good anger. It takes over your life when you do not let go of your anger.

Your feelings are always telling you something. If you feel unhealthy anger, something inside you is not settled, and you need to figure out what's happening.

Anger is a secondary emotion that we feel because it helps us. When you are angry, you feel a little more powerful than when you are in pain. As a result, if you can look at it that way, it is a helpful tool.

Anger also tells you when someone crosses your boundary, which is very important, because if you're upset, you know you should pay attention because something is going on that you do not like. If I ignore that, your feelings will keep getting bigger and bigger.

Anger is a feeling that tries to hide other, more vulnerable feelings from you. These feelings fuel your anger because you got out of the toxic situation, and the abuse stopped. But this did not heal you, and the pain that was caused must be healed for it to stop.

Why Do I Feel Angry?

You might feel angry because what you went through inflicted **core wounds**. By core wounds, I mean that you were made to see yourself differently than what you are at some point.

For example, some of the most common core wounds from narcissistic abuse are beliefs like, "I am bad," or "There is something wrong with me," or perhaps "I'm not good enough; I am not worthy; I am not as good as other people; I do not matter" etc.

So, even though you may know that you are worthy and like who you are today if the core wounds from the past are not healed, they can create feelings of pain, shame, helplessness, and insecurities when these vulnerable feelings come up in our mind.

Anger steps in to protect us from those vulnerable feelings. Anger keeps us focused on the other person, which keeps us from dealing with our feelings.

Anger thinks it is helping you because it makes you focus on the other person. "Look what they did! They did this, and they did that! She said this, and she said that! I cannot believe she did that!" All your anger is focused on the other person, and your brain thinks it is helping you because we are not feeling pain, shame, helplessness, or insecurity.

The problem is that anger makes you more likely to hurt yourself or others by protecting you from those vulnerable emotions.

When you heal those core wounds and acknowledge your past pain, you can start to get back in touch with your true self.

Narcissistic abuse separates you from your true self because you are not allowed to be who you are. This causes much pain, so healing means getting away from the toxic person and then getting back in touch with your true self.

Living in harmony with the beliefs of your authentic self, not the limiting, negative beliefs that the narcissist put into you. This means you have to do the inner work, and sometimes we can think, "God, they did this to me. I have to do so much inner work to heal."

If you think that way, you will not be able to give yourself what you need. If you want to free yourself from your anger, you must be willing to do the inner work.

When you are with a narcissist, you see how angry they are all the time. When victims like you finally get angry about something, they feel bad because they do not want to be like the narcissist. But there is a thin line between **toxic anger** and **healthy anger**.

Healthy Anger

Healthy anger tells you to change, so you should listen to it. But some people do not express their anger because they've seen toxic anger and think, "I am not doing that"; therefore, they contain it. However, containing your anger is also unhealthy.

The goal of healthy anger is to be moderate and to use it to take care of yourself. If we can express our feelings early enough, they will not be explosive and will not be blamed.

The hard part is that most people do not know how to do that without tools. How to see a counselor getting to someone who can help them through this so that they do not hold on to their anger?

I've seen people who have been through it for years and still cannot let go of it. They are stuck in a state of anger and lash out at everyone they see because they cannot control it. That is very common, especially if you are codependent. Codependent people often do not realize they are angry.

We are taught to swallow it and not let it show, and I think in many ways, good girls do not get angry. You do not want to cause a problem or make someone angry, especially if you have done that before. However,

The healthier we get, the more we realize that sometimes we need our anger to stand up for ourselves.

Understanding Your Anger

Ask yourself, "Do I know who I am mad at the most? There is a secondary anger that many people do not see.

For example, if your mother was the abuser and you are so angry at her but you haven't asked yourself, "Why did not my dad protect me?" that is because if dad was the protector, you do not want to be mad at him.

You should not be so much angry that your father did not protect you, but you should be upset that he did not.

This leads us to the fact that many people are angry at themselves. How do they get over being angry at themselves? They always say, "I should not have stayed, I should not have done this, and if I had done that, I would be in a much better place." Their anger hurts them, so how do they get to that point?

Well, for me, it is self-compassion: how can we look at the fact that we did the best we could and why we made those choices we did at the time?

I believe people do better when they learn better because they cannot do what they do not know.

Self-Anger

Being angry at ourselves is something that manifests because you might have done things you are upset about and haven't forgiven yourself for.

If this is the case, we may need to do some work because taking an inventory of how you have hurt others or ourselves will help you let go of those pains and solve the problem.

People who do not get over their anger say things like "he did it, she did it, he did it," and I think you have to get angry in the beginning. It is not a very healthy procedure.

How To Tell When You're Angry

Everyone has different ways of telling when someone is angry. There are three ways to spot anger early:

1. Through physical symptoms.

Most people know that when they are angry: their heart starts to beat faster, their muscles tense up, they might get a headache, and they might clench their jaws.

The emotional signs are the same: it could be low-level irritation, sadness, or fear.

Everyone's anger starts differently, and some people are so stressed out that they do not even notice it.

2. Through behavior

When many people get angry, the first thing they do is point the finger and swear. This is important because the main point is the difference between healthy and unhealthy anger.

But if you focus on yourself and say, "You know what? I am really upset. I need to do something to take care of myself," you are still angry, but it is easier to handle.

3. Through our thoughts

Our thoughts affect how we feel; if you tell yourself, "I am not good, this will never work, I'll never get another relationship," or, even worse, "I have to stay in this one!" of course, you'll feel bad.

But you have to take responsibility for those thoughts and ask yourself, "Is it true that nobody wants me or that I am not a good person?" You must break the negative self-talk cycle that makes you hopeless and angry.

What To Do if You Live With Someone Who Exhibits Toxic Anger?

If you are with someone who experiences toxic anger and you react to it, your anger is valid, but it may not be as much about your past as it is about someone crossing your line or treating you badly.

Your anger is trying to get your attention to tell you that this is not okay with you and that you need to leave because that is sometimes the safest thing you can do in a toxic relationship.

However, leaving does not mean leaving the relationship because many people are not ready to do that. So, instead, leave the room, so you are no longer in that toxic environment.

Therefore, when we get angry, the best thing to do at first is to get away from the situation. This is because until you have more skills, like talking to people and figuring things out, the best idea would be to get away from the situation first and take care of yourself.

Chapter 18:
Should I Forgive Her?

We all have unique understandings of love and forgiveness, and there are numerous ways to describe them.

One of the most difficult tasks you will ever face is forgiving a narcissist. There are numerous misconceptions about what it means to forgive someone, and I believe many people believe that if you forgive someone, you are tacitly accepting their bad behavior. And now you are saying, "Okay, I forgive you." That is not the case.

We do not need to approve of their actions. The damage they've caused is immeasurable, and we will never forgive them. But I've heard all my life that forgiveness is the key. The focus of forgiveness should be on the other person.

Hold on, let me retract that. This has been a constant theme throughout my life. Your well-being and peace of mind are at stake when you forgive. Since I have never fully grasped this concept and have been confused about how one "moves on," allow me to shed some light on the matter.

Forgiveness is personal; it concerns us. That has nothing to do with condoning their behavior or trying to erase the past. It is contrary to the spirit of forgiveness to pretend like the offense never happened.

Hence, the anger and hurt we feel because we haven't forgotten what we need to leave behind.

That is because we did not forgive. If you are having trouble forgiving someone, list their name and the specific offense for five minutes. How do you feel now that you have written that down? It might have brought up feelings like nausea, a lump in your throat, and a trembling voice. Forgiveness can free us from the emotional burden of those memories and serve as a means of overcoming attachment.

Although it may help, forgiveness does not justify wrongdoing. When you forgive someone, you stop letting their actions break your spirit. Is there any sense in that? In the words of Nelson Mandela, "Forgiveness is potent because it sets the spirit free and dispels worry."

There is no such thing as forgiveness for the weak, "This is a quality only found in powerful people," in the words of Gandhi.

These quotes demonstrate that we should abandon that line of reasoning. We need to sever ties with them and take that away from them.

Grace Means Being Able To Forgive

Good fortune is to care about yourself enough to be open and trusting so that you may let go of the suffering associated with any negative experiences. It is putting an end to hurt feelings, and moving on with life is possible via forgiveness. When you let go, you grow. Pent-up

handling everything that comes your way.

I wished for a more stable family unit. The answer was negative for me. We have been through a lot and can forgive the current predicament. A word of advice: do not try to forgive them in front of their face. It is not necessary to tell them this.

Methods of Forgiveness

When you are ready to move past negative sentiments, you must make a sensible and mindful decision. You decide to stop seeing the world through the same lens you always have and let go of your preconceived notions, anger, and victim mentality.

You can tell yourself, "I do not need to get upset about this," and then brush aside whatever bothers you and bring your mood down like it is a bug.

But you can decide that you will not let it destroy you. With practice and persistence, as you begin to heal, it can be as easy as turning a knob.

Admit that this has occurred (I realize this is asking much of you who are still interacting with your narcissist, but I am doing it for you so that tomorrow is a better day for you.

This is not a simple or one-and-done task. You will repeat this process numerous times). Whatever it was that set off an episode, every time it happened, everything was a trigger; you'll know it when you feel it. Accept it, then tell it to leave you alone.

Say, "I appreciate it, but I refuse to let it spoil my day. So today, I choose joy and dwell in a place of forgiveness; I know I am making progress, and I am sure there will be many days when I will feel like I'm losing my mind.

Nonetheless, for the time being, I've decided to forgive my wrongdoers on my terms. I refuse to let anything ruin the rest of my day."

Chapter 19:
What Does Recovery From Narcissistic Abuse Look Like?

I want to bring this up because a client once asked me this question, 'What does it mean to overcome narcissistic abuse?' In my personal opinion, it means letting go of the past, what the narcissist did to you, and how they made you feel.

It would be best if you left that in the past; the narcissist is no longer in your life. You do not want to be with them or miss them anymore. They are no longer a thought in your mind; you have completely moved on with your life, and you have even moved on to the point where you are helping other people overcome narcissistic abuse.

Whether you are a victim or a survivor and thriver, you have moved ahead with your life, learned from your experience, started to engage in self-love and self-care, and focused on yourself.

When you are on the path of recovery, you will feel a lot happier and at peace, and you will no longer experience anxiety anymore. You will be able to wake up and say, "I do not have that stress, I do not feel depressed anymore. I am just content. I am a lot happier than I am now. When I was with the narcissist, I was so miserable, but I think because I wanted to be in a relationship so bad because I wanted to be loved so bad, I think that is why I put up with that."

Then the other thing when it comes to your recovery is setting healthy boundaries and being assertive in your relationships or just with people in general, especially if you struggle with boundaries in your relationships, whether with friends, family, or even romantic relationships. So I go deep into how to do it and how to get over those fears that you may have of people not liking you because you are putting yourself first.

Do not think that if you say no to someone or if you do not go along with this person, or if you concentrate on yourself, they may reject or not like you. You are not exploiting anybody; rather, you are taking care of yourself. You have healthy boundaries, and they deserve to be respected .

The other thing is, one of the stages of recovery is getting help and seeking support, talking to others about it, and taking care of yourself with self-love and self-care.

If you do not recover, you will repeatedly attract narcissists. You do not want to live your life like that! Do not rush your recovery, and do not rush your healing. Instead, overcome narcissistic abuse with proper counseling and help.

What is Rumination?

Rumination is repeatedly thinking the same negative thoughts or trying to mentally solve a problem that cannot be solved. In other words, you are still impacted by the injustice of what has transpired;

you are trying to comprehend what has happened or to come to terms with what has transpired.

The pattern can be upsetting and hard to break. Rumination is simply a sign that you are still in the recovery process.

Please look at it from this perspective. Being around a narcissist shakes everything inside. You might feel like you cannot exist when the narcissist leaves. The turmoil and discomfort the narcissist instilled within you will not disappear until you start changing specific patterns of thoughts and things about yourself.

Think about being lost in a labyrinth with no apparent way out. There are thousands of possible ways out, but you have no idea how to escape. You have a device strapped around your chest. This device is constantly shocking you and giving you uncomfortable signals when you are on the wrong path.

On the other hand, if you are in the right direction, it gives you a pleasant, cozy, warm feeling. There is nothing wrong with feeling uncomfortable or experiencing positive emotions. They indicate whether you are on the right or wrong path.

Ruminations are just an indication that there is still work to be done. When you shift your way of thinking, your perspective changes, and your ruminations fade away, it becomes less bothersome.

Your Path Becomes Clearer the Less You Ruminate

Make sure that you are recovering fully. Take your time to seek that support. Do not be afraid to ask for help. Don't think you could do it on your own because you are strong and independent.

There is nothing wrong with being strong and independent. It is a good thing, but when it comes to your mind, your mental health is everything; it is worth the investment and worth putting in the time, energy, effort, and dedication that you truly deserve to be brand new again to have a better life.

You might feel like you are going to be thinking about this person forever; however, when you develop the strong belief that you do not need to worry about that person and that you no longer need to remind yourself of your anger and pain, this is just as strong as reminding yourself to stop watching their social media. That is how you will walk the path of recovery.

Recovery is all about you knowing yourself and finding out that all the love you need is inside you. There is nothing on the outside that you need that can make you happy that is going to give you love.

When You Show the Narcissist You No Longer Care

Do not forget, the narcissist will go crazy once you start to move on or you show signs of seeing the real them. When you no longer put them on a pedestal or y give them supplies, you are depriving them of what they want: their narcissistic supply.

When they no longer receive their narcissistic supply from you, they will either enter into a rage followed by attempts to chase you, or they will simply move on to the next person. Be warned, they will want to let you go, and that is the sad part.

If you do not remove the narcissist from your life, remember, they are not going to change. They will not say sorry for their actions. You can wait years for the narcissist to realize the error of their ways, but this will never occur. Your life should be firmly in your hands. You will make it through, but do not do it alone.

The End

Author's Note

Dear reader,

I hope you enjoyed my book.

Please don't forget to write a quick review on Amazon. I will personally read it. Positive or negative, I'm grateful for all feedback.

Reviews are so helpful for self-published authors, and your feedback can make such a difference for my book!

Thanks very much for your time, and I look forward to hearing from you soon.

Yours sincerely,

Melanie

About the Author

Melanie Parker is an author and life coach who focuses on writing about relationships, personal growth, and thrive after emotional abuse. After her own personal experience with manipulative people, she now wants to help others with recognizing the symptoms and begin their journey to recovery.

As an avid reader, she was inspired to writing her own books to share her passion for helping others and encourage them to reach their full potential. Her books give actionable advices and true strategies on how to recognize and overcome abusive relationships.

Melanie strives to empower people to let go of limitations and break free from feeling of helplessness, encouraging positive change in the way they understand others and live their own lives.

Made in the USA
Monee, IL
09 July 2023

38908830R00095